"Michelle Gielan is one of the brightest stars in positive psychology and an eloquent champion for rethinking the way we communicate—at work, in our lives, and especially in the media. In *Broadcasting Happiness*, she draws on the latest science and her own experience in the news business to passionately argue that by telling more positive stories and giving the full picture of what's actually happening in our world, we can create a ripple effect that can truly make a difference in people's lives." **—ARIANNA HUFFINGTON**

"*Broadcasting Happiness* is a truly exceptional book, one that will help you to be better and more effective in work and life right away. Michelle Gielan's book is filled with compelling stories, novel research, and practical tips."
—TOM RATH, *New York Times* bestselling author of *Strengths Based Leadership* and *Eat Move Sleep*

"*Broadcasting Happiness* is an inspiring book on radically rethinking the way we communicate with others. Michelle Gielan is a gifted storyteller, and she shares powerful science and practical insights for improving the world around us."
—ADAM GRANT, Wharton professor and *New York Times* bestselling author of *Give and Take*

"*Broadcasting Happiness* taps into our power as individuals to lead collective positive change simply by altering the way we view and share our everyday experiences. Michelle Gielan is a transformative thought leader and her book will change the way you work, live, and look at the world around you."
—BETSY KORONA, Senior Producer, MSNBC

The Science of Igniting and Sustaining
Positive Change

BROADCASTING
HAPPINESS

MICHELLE GIELAN

BenBella Books, Inc.
Dallas, TX

"Still I Rise" from AND STILL I RISE by Maya Angelou, copyright © 1978 by Maya Angelou. Used by permission of Random House, an imprint and division of Penguin Random House LLC. All rights reserved.

BenBella Books, Inc.
10300 N. Central Expressway, Suite #530
BenBella Dallas, TX 75231
www.benbellabooks.com
Send feedback to feedback@benbellabooks.com

Printed in the United States of America
10 9 8 7 6 5 4 3 2 1

Library of Congress Cataloging-in-Publication Data
Gielan, Michelle.
  Broadcasting happiness : the science of igniting and sustaining positive change / Michelle Gielan.
      pages cm
  Includes bibliographical references and index.
  ISBN 978-1-941631-30-0 (hardback)—ISBN 978-1-941631-31-7 (electronic) 1. Organizational behavior. 2. Business communication. I. Title.
  HD58.7.G544 2015
  658.4'06—dc23
                          2015015382

Editing by Glenn Yeffeth and Vy Tran
Copyediting by Francesca Drago
Proofreading by Chris Gage and Michael Fedison
Text design and composition by Sarah Dombrowsky
Cover design by Faceout Studio
Printed by Lake Book Manufacturing

Distributed by Perseus Distribution
www.perseusdistribution.com

To place orders through Perseus Distribution:
Tel: (800) 343-4499
Fax: (800) 351-5073
E-mail: orderentry@perseusbooks.com

Significant discounts for bulk sales are available. Please contact Glenn Yeffeth at glenn@benbellabooks.com or (214) 750-3628.

To our son, Leo Achor,
who broadcasted love
even before finding the words.
He broke open my heart,
making me love the rest of the world
more deeply than ever before.

CONTENTS

INTRODUCTION

I knew something was wrong, but I was on a meteoric rise.

In the midst of going from anchoring a local news broadcast in El Paso, Texas, to hosting two national news programs at CBS News in New York, I saw something while reporting on the south side of Chicago that would eventually change my life's story.

It was the sixth funeral I'd covered in as many months. But this one was different. It was a funeral for a child: A ten-year-old girl had been shot by a stray bullet from gang gunfire at her own birthday party.

As a news reporter, I knew the formula to use to tell the story. I had told this story countless times before. It was a sensational one of random violence, full of raw emotion from family members, which would leave viewers shocked and fearful that this could happen to their loved ones too. And just like many viewers, I didn't know if I should feel numb to the violence or terrified at every moment that life could randomly and irrevocably be destroyed.

I was tired of it. As I sat in that church in Englewood, one of the roughest neighborhoods of Chicago, I was surrounded by a black congregation that was tired too. Yet amidst the emotional exhaustion there were stories of hope, and *those* stories changed the trajectory of my life.

As I listened to the preacher and watched the violence-ravaged congregation surround the grieving mother and sway together to songs of prayer, I realized that the story we often told on the news—a sensational tale of yet one more act of gang violence stealing our kids from us—was only one of the possible stories we could choose to tell. It was one that paralyzed the community instead of rallying everyone together for action. I thought, what would the ripple effect be if we were to focus on the other possible stories unfolding that day?

We could tell the story of a mom surrounded by a loving community that supported her in a time of great challenge.

We could talk about how, despite this tragic act of violence, according to the stats, Englewood was slowly becoming a better place to live, thanks to specific coordinated efforts by the police, community leaders, and local residents.

Instead of focusing solely on the pain and desperation, the story could also highlight the hope, optimism, and resilience of this community. These were all equally true facts.

It was clear to me that there was a better way for us to tell stories, but I had my sights set on a national news position in New York. It was a job I landed two years later—right as the economy collapsed. From my anchor desk at CBS News, I covered the greatest economic downturn in the United States since the Great Depression. We told heart-wrenching stories of the destruction of people's lives as they lost their homes, jobs, and retirement savings. And the sad stories didn't end with the economy. The lights hanging above a multimillion-dollar studio shone down on me as I described in detail how five million barrels of oil devastated the Gulf of Mexico and its surrounding communities.

On July 17, 2010, I left.

It was not because we were telling negative stories or because of the long hours and early mornings. And it wasn't lost on me what I would be giving up—broadcasting to millions of people every time that red light went on over the camera.

I left because I had seen another light. This book is about that story.

Throughout this book, you'll see what I saw over the course of the five years that followed my leaving CBS. You'll see how people can change the trajectory of their families, companies, and communities when they change the stories they communicate. How a single leader at a massive national insurance company changed the way his team thought about its work and *tripled* revenues. How a news series focused on fostering happiness during the recession, which didn't mention a single negative story, got the highest viewer response of the year. How a pair of estranged brothers, each facing the threat of losing his home, reunited to live together. How managers at a certain company trained their brains to experience 23 percent fewer negative effects of high stress. How a school district raised its graduation rate from 44 to 89 percent in a few short years—and how it's not done improving yet. How a two-minute habit can change someone from being a lifelong pessimist into an optimist. How shifting their mindset about getting older can scientifically alter the aging process for a group of seventy-five-year-old men. How a forward-thinking media mogul is using positive research to transform news coverage. And how *you* can use all of the incredible research from positive psychology and the phenomenal stories in this book to better *your* life.

I didn't stop being a broadcaster when I left CBS. I learned that we are all broadcasters, and by changing the stories we transmit, we can create positive change.

We do it by broadcasting happiness.

THE VALUE OF BROADCASTING HAPPINESS

am a happiness researcher. But I didn't start out that way.

In fact, I am a computer engineer with a specialty in electrical engineering and systems architecture—who just wanted to be on TV.

My dream was to become a network news anchor broadcasting from New York City. The reality is that you don't start your career in New York. You start anywhere they'll take you.

Realizing that, I sent one-hundred fifty tapes to news stations around the country. I got *one* call.

"*Bienvenidos á El Paso!*" I heard on the other end of the line, and I packed my bags for Texas. I worked such an awesome schedule there; it led me to ponder some deep philosophical questions, including: If you start your newscast at 3 A.M., do you begin with "*Buenas noches*" or "*Buenos días*"?

I would like to say that my rise to media prominence was due to my hard-hitting investigative stories in El Paso. But that would not quite be accurate. Some of my top stories included "Bed Bugs Invading Your Mattress," "Skin-Eating Fish DO Make for a Better Pedicure," and there was, of course, my biting interview with the Dalai Llama—I mean, "Dolly the Llama." Yes, that interview went down at a petting zoo.

But because of some luck and determination, a year later I found myself in Chicago, covering city hall, and doing an investigative series on alleged police brutality. Because of that work, a short time after that I was sitting in the anchor chair at CBS News in New York City.

I was over the moon and thankful every morning for what I knew was a one-in-a-million dream job. CBS News is an incredible place to work to effect large-scale change. I anchored two early morning news programs and did reports for *The Early Show*—more recently named *CBS This Morning* with Charlie Rose and Oprah's best friend, Gayle King. My office was down the hall from Andy Rooney. Katie Couric would often stop by the studio. I met and interviewed newsmakers, politicians, and celebrities like Sarah Jessica Parker, Donald Trump, and Deepak Chopra. For most of the time I was at CBS News, I was given more airtime than any other anchor or reporter. And every time the red light went on over the camera, I was broadcasting to *millions* of people. I was one grateful former computer programmer.

But within weeks of getting to that anchor desk, the economy tanked. All of a sudden the news cycle became overtaken with heart-wrenching economic stories in addition to the usual reports of murder, death, and destruction. Morning after morning we watched as families lost their homes during the recession and ended up on the streets. We heard about single mothers-of-three who couldn't keep their jobs and were sinking deeper and deeper into debt. About couples in their seventies whose retirement accounts had been decimated and who were falling behind on paying their basic medical bills. Over and over, our mornings began with helplessness and hopelessness. It was painful to watch, especially from a dark news studio, on repeat all day long.

Our choice to continually broadcast stories of *un*happiness is why viewers stopped watching—or at least many of them did. When I ask in my talks at companies and schools how many people have decreased the amount of news they watch because of the negative effect it has on mood—theirs or their family's—often more than 50 percent of the audience members raise their hands. And there is ample science to prove why.

A study I conducted with researchers Dr. Martin Seligman, Dr. Margaret Kern, and Lizbeth Benson from the University of Pennsylvania found that it takes just minutes to dramatically shift someone's mood from neutral to negative simply with news reports.[1] A barrage of negative news reports shows us stories of a world that is frightening and seemingly hopeless. Often these feelings linger with viewers and cascade into their time at work or school. The results of another study show that people who watch local news view their city as significantly more dangerous than it actually is, in terms of anticipated amounts of crime or likelihood of disaster.[2] Given this research, decreasing news consumption can be a form of self-preservation . . . but it has a cost.

My niece Ana, at the time six years old, once complained when I came over to her house that she had been "*ostrich*cized" to her room all afternoon. The fact that both of her parents went to Harvard explains why she uses such big words. (My husband, who also went to Harvard, says, "The fact that they later went to Yale is why she misuses them.") But the more I think about it, the more I think that it is the *perfect* word. In many ways, *ostrich*cized is what largely negative news stories have done to you and me. To preserve a modicum of happiness, we oftentimes stick our heads in the sand, hoping that the negativity in the world will never touch our lives. I don't endorse turning a blind eye to the negative, but I understand feeling overwhelmed by it. But we just can't live our lives *ostrich*cized. Ignorance of the negative does us, and the world, no good.

Henry David Thoreau once said, "There are a thousand hacking at the branches of evil to one who is striking at the root." We can get frustrated about all the negative things going on in our world, but unless we go to the root, we are fighting a losing battle. One of the major roots of the world's challenges is the belief that change is not possible. In fact, the majority of negative news on TV and in our lives feeds us the lie that outcomes are not affected by our behavior. Of course, the reality is that there are millions of things we cannot control, but the problem is when we think *all* things are out of our control.

My epiphany came when I realized that what's happening with the news was *not* a problem of merely too many negative stories. The deeper problem was that we were also telling many of the stories *in the wrong way*, just as we did when reporting on the little girl's death back in Chicago. The lens through which we were broadcasting and viewing many of the stories was distorted. And the trap journalists often fall into is the same one that you and I can get caught in as we lead our families, teams, and organizations through hard times.

While we may complain about the news—its negativity and story selection—in truth we are all broadcasters, and our family, friends, coworkers, and even the strangers we meet are our viewers. We have the same power as journalists. Our brains are constantly selecting stories and transmitting them to others. The things we choose to talk about during the course of our day to our colleagues, friends, and family have a direct influence not only on their mood but also on how they respond to stress, change, and challenges. Everything about our broadcast can paralyze or activate another person's ability to create and sustain positive change.

Each of you reading this may have different audiences in mind. Some of you want to change the way your work teams think about challenge. Some are thirsty for research on how to positively influence your children's trajectories. Some are feeling overwhelmed as an optimist in a pessimistic culture and are looking for tools. But regardless, the conclusion is the same: *You are a broadcaster, which comes with a great deal of power and responsibility.*

I had a hunch that it was not just the ratio of negative to positive news that mattered but also how we told the stories. I am a scientist and engineer, so my first thought was to test this hypothesis on one of the biggest stages of all—at CBS News in New York. The result of my experiment was the highest viewer response of the entire year.

ACTIVATING NEWS, WATCHING THE RIPPLE EFFECT

One time I was at a fancy-schmancy New York bar, Gilt, and a slick banker with an obnoxious Burberry pocket square cornered my friend and me and attempted to impress us by trying to be the world's foremost expert on . . . everything, including news media.

"Let me tell you ladies, happy news doesn't sell. Trust me. Don't waste your time. The proof is in the fact that almost *all* of the news shows are negative. People want the negative. We are addicted, and negativity is our drug. And that's why we drink." His cognac-infused soliloquy went on and on, but the sentiment was clear, and it is often shared by much more thoughtful people.

So when I first pitched the idea of doing a series called "Happy Week" to my most open-minded producer, I wasn't surprised when he initially looked at me like I was suggesting an exposé on the mating habits of French guinea pigs. (And we had already done *that* story.) But here was my idea: In the middle of one of the darkest times in American economic history, let's showcase happiness. Let's bring in experts from the field of positive psychology, which is the scientific study of happiness and human potential, to give practical advice on how to find happiness in the face of big challenges, namely the recession. Since my mentor and subsequent research partner, Dr. Martin Seligman, founded the field in 1998, the body of research that has emerged has turned positive psychology into an essential science-based tool for optimal living, *especially for leaders* in every organization, family, and community.

During Happy Week, our aim was not to ignore the reality of the economic collapse. We wanted to talk about ways to foster more happiness in the *midst* of it and not wait helplessly until it was over. We wanted an activated, wholehearted, solutions-focused approach to broadcasting news. Our forward-thinking producer agreed to give it a shot.

We got more positive emails from viewers as a result of that week of programming alone than we did for the entire year prior. I read email after email from viewers who said that those segments made them realize they had control of their happiness, and that even in the middle of the hardest economic challenges of their lifetime, they could take positive steps to create change.

One viewer from Oklahoma wrote in, and his story still makes me emotional. His home, like many others, was facing foreclosure. He wrote that he had not talked to his brother, who lived a mere twenty-five miles away, for the past twenty years. They had fought over money and cut off contact. He had recently heard that his brother's home was facing foreclosure as well, and after seeing the segment on CBS on rethinking financial stresses, he decided to reach out to him. The two men ended up pooling resources to save one of their homes and moved in together! Each was now very happy to not only have a roof over his head but also his formerly estranged brother by his side. This story was one of many that showed how people are propelled to take positive action when they experience even the smallest mindset shift, and what results is a new reality.

6

Stories like this one from those Oklahoma brothers prompted me to walk away from a broadcast journalist's dream job to get an advanced degree in Applied Positive Psychology from the University of Pennsylvania, working under Professor Martin Seligman who founded the field. Inspired by what I learned, I cofounded the Institute for Applied Positive Research (IAPR) in order to connect thinkers from Harvard, Yale, Columbia, and the University of Pennsylvania to study outliers who are able to motivate people through effective communication.

My cofounder is Shawn Achor, whom many of you know as a famous Harvard-trained researcher, speaker, and *New York Times* best-selling author of multiple books on the connection between happiness and success. But my favorite of his credentials is that he's now my husband. Some of the greatest moments of my life that have propelled the most growth have been serendipitous and unexpected. Meeting Shawn was one. Meeting Arianna Huffington at the perfect time was another.

A week after I finished the near-final draft of the manuscript for this book, all that earlier work from CBS and UPenn came to fruition in a very unexpected way. On a wintry morning in 2015 in New York City's Soho, Shawn and I were invited to the home of Arianna Huffington—cofounder and editor-in-chief of the *Huffington Post*. During the course of that morning, we realized that we had been on the exact same mission to transform journalism. The *Huffington Post*'s fantastic What's Working initiative to highlight positive, solutions-focused stories is a prototypical example of what I call "Transformative Journalism" that a decade of research in positive psychology had proven was necessary to create positive change. (See also the appendix: The Journalist Manifesto.)

In her book *Thrive*, Arianna provides a compelling case for rethinking our definition of success and its relationship to our well-being. Applying that enlightened thinking to journalism, she now argues that our *collective* well-being hinges in large part on the way the news media reports the news. I was also thrilled to learn that Arianna is one of those rare thought leaders who actually live what they preach. Her approach is courageous; she is leading the charge to transform media based on the broadcasting-happiness research at a time when doing so runs counter to industry practices and when the obsession with sensational, negative news coverage is at an all-time high.

The moment Arianna heard about the research Shawn and I had been doing at the IAPR to test the impacts of Transformative Journalism on everything from mood to cognitive ability to business outcomes, she called the editorial director of the *Huffington Post*, Danny Shea, to race over to her place to join us for the discussion. Danny is the kind of person who is three steps ahead in a conversation, seeing the implications and cutting through the clutter to get to actionable ideas. I liked him immediately.

Together we designed a partnership between the IAPR and the *Huffington Post* that would create a compelling research-based argument to journalists, news executives, and advertisers on the value of supporting activating, engaging, solutions-focused journalism. The results of studies will be available to the public (check out BroadcastingHappiness.com), so everyone can see if watching positive news stories before going to work improves sales and customer service, if watching negative news impairs cognitive abilities and creative problem solving, if watching transformative stories improves one's athletic performance at the gym, and if educating journalism students about how to create optimism inoculates them against the cynicism pervading some of the industry. Arianna has predicted zeitgeists before, and we are fully confident she has done it again. In fact, the cultural shift has already begun—and this one has the potential to transform society in ways we have never seen before.

Ultimately, though, this book is not about me or my institute or even the power of the news media. It is about you. It is about the power we all have to ignite and create positive change. By changing the way we *all* communicate, we can make the people around us at work, at home, and in our communities believe that their behavior matters and therefore see a path forward. This book is about how *you* can be the person who consciously influences others for the better.

YOU ARE A BROADCASTER

Since leaving my anchor chair, I have come to three main conclusions, gleaned from all the research and the work we have done at organizations around the globe:

1. *The vision of reality we see and share changes other people and can move them from paralysis to activation.* The stories we tell about the world predict whether we believe that happiness is a choice and whether we'll take action to create happiness—or stay stagnant, inert, and powerless. Our stories are a reflection of our mindset or outlook on a situation and stem from the way we synthesize the facts we gather from the world around us. Positive, optimistic, solution-focused stories, even if they start in the midst of challenging circumstances, fuel hope and inspire others to believe that change is possible and that our behavior matters. Changing our story from one of paralysis to activation amplifies our power to inspire other people and ignite positive change.

2. *Our stories are predictive not only of happiness but also of business, educational, and health outcomes, including engagement, intelligence, energy, and profitability.* New research from the fields of positive psychology and neuroscience shows that small shifts in the way we communicate internally and with others can create big ripple effects on business outcomes, including 31 percent higher

productivity,[3] 25 percent greater performance ratings,[4] 37 percent higher sales,[5] and 23 percent lower levels of stress.[6] Using scientifically supported communication strategies to ripple out a positive mindset can increase happiness and success at work for others as well as for ourselves, instantly making us more effective leaders.

3. *We are all broadcasters.* We constantly broadcast information to others, even if we don't say a word. Managers broadcast to their teams during meetings about potential new business opportunities within the industry. Team members broadcast to one another about the likelihood of success on a project. Clients broadcast to potential clients about a company's customer service. Parents broadcast to their children about how to look at the challenges they experience at school. Even introverts broadcast their reactions to what other people are saying through their nonverbal communication. And the messages we choose to broadcast shape others' views of the world and how they operate within it. But before we can influence others, it is crucial to see in the first place how powerful we are to do just that.

THE POWER TO INFLUENCE

MINDSET AND THE MEN

The story you hear about aging is simple. After thirty, your body degenerates as you age. You are on a trajectory toward decreased ability and attractiveness. The end.

But that story is scientifically inaccurate. It would be more accurate to say that the story you believe *and* tell about aging could change even something as seemingly intractable and incontrovertible as the aging process. And if we can change that, what else can we change? Let me explain more fully.

The brilliant maverick Harvard professor Dr. Ellen Langer has been designing studies for four decades that prove our mental story affects our health. In a single study Dr. Langer cracked the code and scientifically reversed signs of aging. She did not accomplish this with expensive creams or plastic surgery but simply by telling a different story about aging. This happened almost three decades ago, but it still has yet to be learned by the general public.

"Welcome to the year 1959!" Dr. Langer said in 1979, as she invited a group of seventy-five-year-old men to go on a weeklong retreat as part of a large-scale psychology experiment.[7] The men had been told one thing only before coming to the retreat: They could not bring any newspapers, photographs, or books from the past twenty years of their lives. Langer and her team took these men twenty years back in time to the late fifties by refitting the retreat center with items recalling the year 1959, when these men were fifty-five years old, such as *Saturday Evening Post*s and *Life* magazines. Each man received a badge with his name on it and a photo of himself from 1959. They were told to talk only about their jobs and lives from that time period.

Langer had a daring hypothesis: The human aging process was mediated by what we tell ourselves about our life stories. And this seemingly off-the-wall study showed she was right. Langer tested the men for signs of aging before and after the week, and the results were mind-blowing. After one week of reliving life in their mid-fifties, the men showed, on average, statistically significant improvements in strength, posture, flexibility, memory, and intelligence. Even more incredible, the men's eyesight improved by an average of 10 percent! Even naive raters—people who had never met the men—viewed pictures of the men at week's end and judged them as looking an average of three years younger.

For more information on this incredible study, Dr. Langer has a fantastic book called *Counterclockwise*, which shows over and over that our perceptions of the world around us—our personal beliefs and the stories we tell ourselves—drive our health.

This study is one of many in a burgeoning field of research that shows how changing our mindset can improve not only our bodies but also our sense of humor, intelligence, athletic ability, sales prowess, and energy. These elderly men had slowed or reversed many of the effects of aging after adopting a different mental outlook for just one week. Imagine the impact that practicing an energetic, youthful, and wise mindset today could have on your life as you break from the normal expectations for your age. The study successfully shows that we can live healthier, happier, and longer lives simply by thinking differently—in this case revitalized with youth and happiness.

Stop for a moment to think about how much Langer's research changes everything. Studies show that a change in story and mindset—thinking of yourself as a confident person—can enable people to perceive you as having more confidence.

Social psychologist and associate professor at Harvard Business School Amy Cuddy has found that by simply looking the part, by using a "high-power pose" to tell a nonverbal story for two minutes, you can drop your levels of the stress hormone cortisol by about 25 percent and raise levels of testosterone by 20 percent.[8] Additionally, naive raters will, on average, view you as better performing and more likely to be hired.[9] If you mentally conceive of yourself as grateful, you might see more miracles in your life as your brain scans the environment for things to be grateful for. If you see yourself as an agent of change, you increase your power to create social influence. Mindset, it turns out, is the key to broadcasting a positive message to the world.

And if you help others to see that positive change is possible, empowered action becomes the logical next step.

THE PRESIDENT WHO HATED HAPPINESS

The first time he heard about the research on happiness and its link to success, he called it "fluff." But very quickly Gary Baker, president of Nationwide Brokerage Solutions, formerly Insurance Intermediaries Inc. (III), a Nationwide company, changed his story. And his new story tripled his company's revenues from three hundred fifty million to more than a billion dollars and serves as a case study for other companies around the world, including Google, US Foods, and T-Mobile.

Using happiness research was a big change for Baker's wholly owned subsidiary of Nationwide Insurance. His company had fallen into the same trap that ensnares much of corporate America: "If you are having fun or enjoying your work, you must not be working hard enough. Hit your numbers and then we'll all be happy." This societal norm, or "social script," has created internal conflict at work for many of us because it goes against our nature. Science has shown that when we are filled with positive emotions, our brains actually work much better and our results improve.[10] Instinctively we may know that the negative social script puts us at odds with our most human instincts—and that creates stress and an epidemic of disengagement. But because the desire to conform is incredibly strong, most of us give in and slowly disengage from our work too.

In 2010, our team at GoodThink, in partnership with the International Thought Leaders Network (ITLN), developed a positive psychology–based workshop called The Orange Frog and began a massive rollout at Nationwide. The aim of the program, based on a business parable about an orange frog named Spark, was to help the organization confront and rewrite social scripts that were not serving success, and provide a narrative pathway for people to reach a more positive mindset, attain higher levels of optimism, and deepen social connections. Through the stories of the various frogs in the parable, employees learn the best practices of resilient leaders, become more adaptive, and develop a capacity to "see" more opportunities, which all lead to better business outcomes. Together with ITLN, we trained thousands of employees at Nationwide how to put the latest happiness research into practice to achieve tangible business results, and it didn't take long before Baker and his team saw the effects.

Baker, while initially against "fluffy" happiness research, is a man driven by data and results. When he saw his company's revenues triple after the Orange Frog training and the largest improvement in engagement scores across all of Nationwide Insurance, he changed his story. He also changed the walls in his office, painting the entire call center bright orange. The once somber cubicles are now scattered with orange plush frogs, and hanging around the offices are large framed pictures of employees working at soup kitchens wearing bright orange shirts. Employees are very enthusiastic about "being orange." They know broadcasting happiness can fuel their success.

The changes did not stop there. Now at the Nationwide Sales Academy, as salespeople are initiated, they are taught a story that is different from the usual corporate social script: Happiness leads to sales, not the other way around. With permission to broadcast happiness, many other leaders in the company changed their stories and practices as well, including Nationwide Insurance COO Mark Pizzi.

For years, when Pizzi entered his Columbus office he often would think about or write down reasons he was grateful for his job and life. But now that publicly practicing happiness is central to the company's approach, he also occasionally gets on Yammer (Nationwide's internal social media) to broadcast his gratitudes to the company's employees. His hope is that practicing gratitude will inspire others to adopt a similar positive habit.

"I have to work at it; I am no different than anyone else," Pizzi explains. "The boldness with which we act to rebuild people's lives, and our business results, ties in to how we think. We want to embed positivity into Nationwide's DNA."

The leaders at Nationwide accomplished this by reassessing the stories they broadcast to employees and rewriting the ones that work against their individual and collective success.

I often share these stories and other business cases in the talks I give at companies around the world, and invariably someone asks the question that is on the minds of many in the room: "These people are leaders of big organizations. Of course they can influence others. But what about me, or my colleagues, who don't lead teams? I mean, really, what could we possibly do?" It's a fair question, which has popped up so many times that, eventually, I began addressing it before it was posed. The "I'm *just* a [insert title here]" is another example of a social script that works against us. It's a story that says you are powerless. It's a story that is false. More accurately, it is a story that does not have to remain true.

Change your story, change your power. I have seen countless examples of how you don't need to be in a traditional position of power to broadcast happiness and be successful at sparking positive change.

You can transform the way people think about work, and create both business and social change, no matter what level of the organization you're at. Numerous examples are shared throughout this book. As a matter of fact, of the case studies described herein, the lion's share do not feature those in the C-suite but rather normal people like you and me. Even at Nationwide, the person who actually had the biggest ripple effect was "Sparkette," a female employee in Learning and Development who, with the help of one of those orange plush frogs, was able to get a positive story to go viral in less than thirty seconds. Her story will come later on. But first, let's learn about a woman on a mission to shift the story being told about her neighborhood. It was the same community I mentioned at the beginning of this book.

REWRITING A BAD REP

Thinking about the amount of crime in Englewood overwhelmed me. For years, the vast majority of the stories told about this Southside Chicago neighborhood have been crime-related. A quick Google search of "Englewood Chicago" produces a plethora of articles about guns and murder, including a website that tracks homicides by block. And that can leave anyone feeling like a revival of this once-blossoming neighborhood would be impossible . . . so why try?

Rashanah Baldwin knew there was another story to tell about her community. I got to know her during her internship at FOX News Chicago. She shadowed me to learn how to conduct interviews and write scripts—but through that process I learned from her as well, especially about the value of telling often-untold inspiring stories from forgotten parts of the city. She already knew at the time that even though she was "just a girl from the 'hood," she wanted to work on rewriting the stories people were telling about it. Her hope was to motivate fellow residents and government officials to believe in her neighborhood and make a greater investment in it. Baldwin said, "I'm trying to convince people that there is hope here and [that] it is a place where you can raise a family."[11]

On a trip to Chicago in 2014, I saw Baldwin smiling back at me from the front page of the *Chicago Tribune*. She was featured for her work spreading positive stories about Englewood. The article was about "What's Good in Englewood," a media campaign she began as a way to tell some of Englewood's best stories. Baldwin has her own radio program, appears on TV segments, and uses the hashtag #goodinenglewood on social media to broadcast positive reports, including high school students who were awarded Gates Millennium Scholarships, gun buyback programs that work, and job-training classes offered by the community's urban farm organization. And these days she doesn't have to work as hard to uncover the positive news; it finds her. Community members use social media to connect with her about inspiring stories they hear from friends and family. Rashanah Baldwin is broadcasting a different side of Englewood, and changing people's minds in the process.

More recently, the movement has gone national. The positive stories have spread far beyond the three square miles of the neighborhood; her efforts were featured in the *Huffington Post*. Even better, when you search "Englewood Chicago" on Google now, on the first page of results among the stories of crime, is a link above the fold that leads to positive stories about the neighborhood.[12]

If Baldwin had stopped at "I'm just . . ." she would never have had the kind of mindset that fueled her to tell the story no one is telling. If she had worried that no one would care about these stories because positive news isn't sexy, she would not have started #goodinenglewood. And if she had thought, "Even if I did do this, no one will get involved in the movement," she would have never seen its potential. But Rashanah Baldwin is a positive broadcaster, and she brought great change—and happiness—to her community.

THE THREE GREATEST PREDICTORS OF SUCCESS

Behind these three seemingly disparate examples are the keys to creating positive growth in every domain of life gleaned from our research in positive psychology. After working with more than one-third of the Fortune 100, we have isolated the three greatest predictors of success at work: work optimism, positive engagement, and support provision. We have since developed a thirty-item metric called the Success Scale, which measures how your brain processes your work and to what degree you are a positive broadcaster.

And excitingly, you can test yourself on these predictors—right now. Before reading the next section, *we invite you to take the assessment on our website for free at BroadcastingHappiness.com (use the code "ichoosehappiness")*. It will inform your understanding of the rest of the book, so I encourage you to take a few minutes to try it. You'll receive your personal scores and an interpretive report.

Taken together the results of these measures are amazingly accurate predictors of success at work, and knowing these can give you a strong indication of how someone will perform. As a matter of fact, our research has shown that together these measures from the Success Scale account for as much as 75 percent of job successes. (So, considering that employees are often hired based on grades and technical skills, perhaps it's time to rethink that formula.)

WORK OPTIMISM: "GOOD THINGS HAPPEN"

On the Success Scale, "work optimism" measures where you devote your mental resources—that is, if you're focused more on the paralyzing or energizing aspects of work—and how strongly you believe good things will happen, which includes not only your own successes but also those of your colleagues and your organization. As a Work Optimist, you are five times less likely to burn out than a pessimist and three times more likely to be highly engaged in your jobs. You are also significantly more likely to get along with coworkers. If you score in the top quartile as a Visionary Work Optimist, compared to normal Work Optimists, you're two times as likely to be highly engaged at work and three times as likely to be extremely satisfied with your jobs.

Research from the field of positive psychology shows that when we are rationally optimistic, we are more successful at work. At our research institute we call this the "happiness advantage," and any of you who have read Shawn Achor's book of the same title will know all the ways that happiness fuels success. In short, when we are able to take a realistic assessment of the present moment while maintaining a belief that our behavior matters in the face of challenges, we achieve better results at whatever we are doing. For instance, doctors who are positive-minded come up with the correct diagnosis 19 percent faster than doctors who are neutral.[13] In a large-scale experiment done at MetLife, optimistic salespeople outsold their pessimistic counterparts by 37 percent.[14] For managers, this study single-handedly demonstrates the importance of including optimism at or near the top of the list of job requirements when hiring.

Other studies have shown that if you think of a happy memory ahead of standardized testing, you'll do better. Happiness and positivity even influence our health and longevity. In short, cultivate happiness and you're cultivating success at the same time. Positive broadcasters do that for themselves and others.

POSITIVE ENGAGEMENT:
"IN THE FACE OF CHALLENGES,
I CAN SUCCEED"

Positive engagement measures your response in the face of stressful situations. In other words, this measures your story about stress. Those considered Engagement Masters on the Success Scale, who fall into the top quartile, perceive and broadcast the idea that stress is "a challenge as opposed to a threat," and their brains become activated in the face of setbacks. As an Engagement Master, you are fifteen times less likely to burn out than those workers who feel helpless and six times more likely to be highly engaged with your work. You are two times as likely as all others to perform your assigned duties well, three times more likely than all others to be satisfied with your jobs, and three times more likely than all others to contribute to the company.

In a study done at UBS, a global financial services firm, researchers from our institute and from Yale University found that with a simple three-hour training, stressed-out managers could change the story and learn a new way to deal with stressful situations—and the effects were nothing short of incredible.[15] The leaders who went through a Rethinking Stress training, which taught them how to change their mindset about stress, experienced a 23 percent drop in stress-related symptoms, like headaches, backaches, and fatigue, as compared to the control group. And that drop occurred during the busiest tax season to date! Positive broadcasters understand how to rethink stresses in their own lives and broadcast that engaged mindset to others so that they too believe they can succeed in the face of challenges.

SUPPORT PROVISION: "I INVEST IN THE SUCCESS OF OTHERS"

Support provision on the Success Scale measures how much support you provide to others at work. It may sound counter-intuitive—in order to be successful, shouldn't you be the one receiving support? Interestingly, knowing how much you give instead of receive is much more predictive of your success at work. This metric assesses how likely you are to step in to help others when they may be falling behind in their work or need a listening ear. As a Work Altruist, that is, those who score in the top quartile for the support provision, you are five times less likely to burn out than those in the bottom quartile. You are much more engaged at work and 65 percent of you can expect a promotion in the next year! These numbers are the scientific proof that when you give, you get.

Social support is the greatest predictor of happiness that exists. For many people, having a handful of meaningful relationships is the surest path to happiness. Creating an environment at work that supports a positive, bridge-building culture drives success in a way that is infectious and cumulative. Positive broadcasters are able to nurture cultures at the office that support individual and team success and cause positive behaviors to go viral, creating an upward spiral of success.

THE SEVEN KEYS TO BEING A TRANSFORMATIONAL BROADCASTER

Anyone can become a broadcaster and learn how to communicate in a way that motivates others and produces results. Based on the latest research from the fields of positive psychology, social psychology, and neuroscience, and my extensive media training, I have developed the following seven practical strategies to help you become a positive broadcaster.

This book is organized around the three principles outlined above. Work optimism, positive engagement, and support provision are the leverage points you can use to influence the mindset and behavior of other people. Move the needle in any of the following three domains and you'll end up impacting individual and team success rates. Many of the examples presented in the following chapters are pulled from the business world, but we'll also look at how to apply the research at school and home to deepen our most important relationships and create environments that promote success.

In **Part I: Capitalize on Positivity**, you'll learn how to develop and leverage an optimistic mindset in yourself and others to fuel success. By starting with **power leads**, I'll teach you how to effectively prime the brain for higher levels of performance and set the social script of your business relationships to positive in order to raise business outcomes, including engagement, productivity, and profitability. In the chapter on repeating success stories to create **flash memories**, I'll share with you how to use past wins as fuel for future successes. You'll learn how to identify and communicate to colleagues about previous accomplishments in a way that drives high performance moving forward. In the chapter on **leading questions**, I'll introduce you to the most effective ways to use questions to drive positive thinking. In my institute's work with our clients, we have seen that when business leaders employ these simple techniques, not only does morale improve but a whole host of business metrics do as well.

In **Part II: Overcome Stress and Negativity**, you'll learn how to boost positive engagement in others by facing stress and negativity the right way. In the chapter on how to **fact-check**, I'll tell you how to help others rethink stressful situations and identify the parts of their reality that are energizing in order to move their brain from paralysis to activation. When faced with negative people, I'll show you that one of the scientifically proven strongest ways to handle them is by engaging in a **strategic retreat**. In that chapter, you'll learn how to make a strategic retreat and then create and execute a victorious reentry plan that will lessen their destructive gravitational field at the office. And in the chapter on the **four Cs**, you'll learn how to deliver bad news better. If done right, bad news can actually create bonds and a deeper sense of connection.

In **Part III: Create a Positive Ripple Effect**, you'll become a master at creating an environment infused with high levels of support provision from everyone, in which positive habits and behaviors can organically spread. In the final chapter, I'll explain how you can make a positive message **go viral**. You'll learn how to spread contagious optimism, spur positive behavioral changes, and shift the culture at work or home from negative or neutral to positive.

For those of you who have ever complained that the news is too negative, the Journalist Manifesto on page 243 is a research-based case showing how the emerging business model in journalism supports the coverage of activating and engaging solution-focused news stories, and why it is a fallacy to believe that negative news sells better than positive. The manifesto reviews exactly how to engage in Transformative Journalism and why it is not only good for society but also good for business. The manifesto contains tools to report the news while simultaneously making this world a better place by engaging with decision makers and the public to create positive action. *I encourage you to read and share the Journalist Manifesto with the*

TV, radio, and digital journalists and outlets that you would like to see cover the news more positively. And more importantly, please share it with reporters, bloggers, and news organizations already engaging in Transformative Journalism, so they fully understand the scientific reasons behind why what they are doing is right and why now is the time to tell even more of those stories. Transformative Journalism is the key to transforming society at large. You can be the broadcaster to point them toward this new model.

While the news media as a whole might not yet be ready to make the great shift, I think we—individuals and organizations—need not wait. As broadcasters ourselves, we can use the same strategies in our own lives to create upward spirals of positive change. Although you might already be broadcasting happiness to some degree, there is always more that can be done, and more importantly, you can activate others to boost their own signals.

The loving, activated response of the community in Englewood, Chicago, during the aftermath of tragedy eventually changed the entire trajectory and story of my life. I believe wholeheartedly that the research and stories in this book can do the same for you. I hope this book will empower you to broadcast happiness and help change the trajectory of the people around you, activating them and showing them that happiness can be a choice. Once we have a positive message, we need to find a way to crank the power to full. That is why I wrote this book, and that is why you are crucial. The world needs more people broadcasting happiness.

PART I

Capitalize on Positivity

Positivity is the world's most underutilized, naturally occurring resource available to fuel success and forward progress. Too often our brains get caught up on all that is broken, forgetting about all that's working. Yet it's exactly those stories of success and triumph—no matter how small—that communicate that not only is positive change possible, it is closer than previously thought. Leverage positivity and optimism to simultaneously activate the people around you and ignite positive change. In Part I, learn the first and most powerful steps you can take to unlock your positive influence as a positive broadcaster.

POWER LEADS

Prime the Brain for High Performance

One Thanksgiving I had such big news to share with my parents that I waited, flying all the way from Boston to Bethesda, Maryland, to tell them in person. I couldn't wait for the "oohs" and "aahs" that you only get from proud parents. As I walked through the door to their home, my father greeted me with the glee I had expected and needed.

"Mooshie-Pooh!" (Yes, that's my nickname.)

My mom gave me a big hug, put the kettle on the stove, and turned to say, "So, what's up in your life? Catch us up on everything!"

My news was not only exciting but potentially life-changing. I had been working for months on a business plan with one of my classmates at college. We had entered it in a business plan competition. The top prize was twenty-thousand dollars in seed money, and three days before the holiday break, I found out we won!

I was midway through taking a full breath to make my pronouncement when my mom started looking at me funny. She tilted her head from side to side like a puppy with a confused look on her face. I stopped midsentence and said, "What?! What are you looking at?"

"I just . . . Danny, come look at Michelle. Do you see that?" She pointed her finger at my eyes. "Doesn't she look a little . . . cross-eyed?"

"Mom, I'm fine." I instantly tried to move the conversation back to my award and away from this eyeball theory that was starting to develop. I had seen how these "medical mysteries" had gone before with my parents.

My attempt failed miserably. A minute later my father had dug out his digital camera to take a picture for the doctor to show how the "muscles" around one of my eyes must be "pulling it" toward my nose. All I could see in his blurry, way-too-close photo were two eyeballs—stunned that after six months of being away from home, this was the welcome I was getting.

This strange start to my visit sparked a cascade of nerve-racking events. First, my father slid me into *his* eye appointment, which he happened to have the next day and to which he always hates going. (Yes. How convenient.) The doctor dilated my eyes during the exam, and since I had left my sunglasses at home, I stumbled down the street in the bright sunshine after the appointment—blind as a bat. I think at one point I had wandered into a back alley because all I could smell was trash. Two-hundred fifty dollars later I found out my eyes were, in fact, perfectly fine.

And I forgot to tell my parents about the award and had to email them from Boston.

My parents' "medical theory" welcome has since become a family joke, but it's a great example of how the start of a social script dictates its trajectory. Rather than receiving elated congratulations, I ended up receiving large amounts of cortisol and lots of eye drops, hijacking a good part of my weekend with them. Beginnings are exceptionally important. And when we start with something negative or stressful, it focuses everyone's attention on that part of our reality, preventing us from using those valuable and finite resources for observing possibilities and celebrating successes.

We see this in business all the time. A senior leader announces potential layoffs by beginning the meeting with something like, "For those of you who haven't heard, things are pretty terrible around here, and we're expecting the situation to get worse before it gets better." This doesn't instill employees with confidence in the leadership or give the assurance that they'll have a job next week. Beginnings are important when we start new projects, update clients on new products, and when we catch up with colleagues around the watercooler. The way we begin these conversations often predicts the level of success that follows. But while the effects of anxiety-producing kickoffs are fascinating, much more interesting is how positive beginnings can affect our brains and business outcomes . . . especially when they involve a couple of cocktails.

COCKTAILS ON NEWBURY

When I was fresh out of college I got a job doing basically two things: writing computer code and watching people sip cocktails. I worked at a software company in Boston that had renovated an old bookstore in a historic building on Newbury Street. Above the entrance were stained-glass windows of the Cheshire Cat, Shakespeare, and other popular literary figures and characters to inspire us to be innovative, though we were using C++ instead of Elizabethan English. My desk faced a window overlooking Newbury Street's fashionable shops and restaurants with patio seating. Envying people having afternoon drinks and lunch was my break from a very high-pressure, highly detail-oriented job.

To be honest my boss scared me. Not because Ellen was mean, though she was demanding, but because every time she decided to stalk through the cubicles, grinning like the afore-mentioned cat above our building's entrance, she would ask me right off the top of our conversation in a caring but serious tone, "What is one awesome thing you did—no matter how small—at work in the past week?"

In the beginning, I couldn't come up with anything. I would panic. Literally all that would pop into my head was "Ummm, I showed up to work?" or "I remembered deodorant?" It was a very simple question, but in order to answer it, my brain had to furiously scan my actions throughout the past week for even the tiniest achievements.

Because I usually just stood there tongue-tied, sweating pro-fusely (thank goodness for the deodorant!), Ellen would offer an answer that she had observed:

"A couple lines of code you wrote last week will be included in the next project build. Good job."

"I saw you stayed late last night to help Darren. Strong work."

"The other day in the pitch meeting you had a small yet very strong idea that we built upon and are going to try out. That was great."

Her simple beginning to all our interactions trained me to look for positive moments from my workday during which my behavior mattered. After working there for just a couple of weeks, I began to automatically catalog small successes so I would be prepared for the next time I saw her. Ellen's simple yet inspira-tional *power lead* caused me to identify meaningful moments in my workday that were valuable and led to my success. Not to mention, it also showed me that someone saw the good in me and cared about my performance. Talk about good fuel at work!

The first key to being a positive broadcaster is starting with a "power lead." The concept of the power lead came from my days in media. The first story that is aired on the news is called the lead. In an effort to attract viewers and increase ratings, there is a formula that has developed in news: Start with the most sen-sational story available to grab the viewers' attention. I'm sure you've heard the expression "if it bleeds, it leads," but that kind of negative lead hijacks our brain and leaves us stressed, with less mental resources to effectively problem solve. Using the power lead takes the opposite approach. Since we know that positiv-ity fuels performance, when we begin meetings, conversations, emails, and other human interactions with a positive lead story, comment, or fact, we reorient the brain toward the parts of our lives that help us create a better reality.

A power lead is a positive, optimistic, and inspiring beginning to a conversation or other communication that sets the tone for the ensuing social script. The power lead is one of the most crucial steps to motivate a team, connect more deeply with colleagues, or set the stage for higher levels of creativity because it helps our brains focus on growth-producing areas. Since humans are socialized to mimic one another, the people you are connecting with often reciprocate the positive nature of a power lead as you continue to connect. Over the course of this chapter, I'm going to show you multiple examples of power leads and how to use them for maximum gain.

What we are first exposed to influences our behavior. In social psychology, we call it priming. Priming can be accom-plished with little words or short phrases, without the person who is being primed even noticing what is going on.

Priming experiments can be fun! In one study, researchers asked participants to take a "language test."[1] During this fake test, they were either exposed to words related to rudeness (eg, *rude, impolite,* and *obnoxious*) or politeness (eg, *polite, respect,* and *considerate*). After the test they were put into a situation, one by one, in which they could be polite or rude—undercover research-ers would intentionally ignore a participant during a group conversation, and the participant could either rudely interrupt the others or politely stand by for the remaining ten minutes of the conversation. Participants who had been exposed to the rude words were nearly 50 percent more likely to interrupt, whereas the majority of the "polite" participants waited the entire ten minutes! This is a great experiment to try with your unruly teen-agers. And if you have young children, you can try out this next experiment and boost their performance.

Four-year-olds who were asked to think of a positive memory versus a negative one were 66 percent more efficient at figuring out games involving shapes.[2] The benefits of priming with positivity show up even during our earliest stages of development!

Research shows that how we begin a conversation is predictive of how well it turns out,[3] and if we know how charismatic a leader is, we've got a strong predictor of his or her team's level of success.[4] Moreover, because the power lead is simple and can come from any person regardless of rank, it can turn anyone, at any level of an organization, into a positive broadcaster. If you are positive and optimistic—and expressive of this mindset— you can motivate others and spark positive change.

A study done in collaboration with the Air Force Research Laboratory found that people do better at their jobs when they have strong, positive leaders at the helm when challenges strike.[5] Additionally, using power leads improves our experience of the world, better preparing us to be a positive broadcaster to others. The Incentive Research Foundation found that people who used a power lead at least once during the course of its three-day event rated their experiences as much more positive than those who did not across all forty-two metrics that were tested.[6] The practice of broadcasting positivity reinforces an optimistic mindset and makes you feel happier. And as mentioned in chapter one, when our brains are focused on the positive, we get the "happiness advantage"—our brains move into the high-performance zone. The power lead primes you and others for positivity in seconds, thereby pushing everyone into that zone before additional time is lost.

In this chapter, you'll learn the science behind why a power lead is so influential in changing business outcomes and shaping our relationships with others, and how using it in key moments fuels others through stressful or challenging times so they become happier and more successful. I'll share concrete examples of how to use the power lead in several domains of life to help make each of us a more positive broadcaster. Whether you're leading team meetings to go through the day's agenda, talking with a stressed colleague who needs your help, or kicking off dinner at home with your family, using the power lead will transform the collective mindset for the better.

THE HAPPIEST WOMAN IN THE WORLD

While developing a positive psychology program with Walmart for its 1.5 million associates, I visited several of its stores to pilot the program. After a morning meeting with store employees, one in particular, Sharon, came up to me and declared that we should study her because she is the "happiest person you will ever meet." She had a big smile on her face and carried herself with nothing short of exuberance. She was warm, infectiously positive, and when she laughed, her whole body got into it. Talk about a good power lead! I smiled back and asked her how we can be sure that she is the world's most positive person, and that's when Sharon told me a story I would not forget.

Sharon had met the man of her dreams a bit later in life, got married, and was blissfully content. Just a few months after the wedding, her mother, with whom she was extremely close, died suddenly of unexpected health problems. Her loving husband helped her through six month of grieving. Just as she was starting to feel like her normal self again, he was suddenly killed in a car accident. I was dismayed. This wasn't proof of happiness like I expected. Seeing the shock on my face, Sharon said the reason she has the right to call herself the happiest woman on the planet is that despite all of those circumstances, every day she has made a conscious choice to not only be positive but also to share it with others.

Sharon greets her fellow associates with warm smiles or high fives when she first sees them. They love her, even when they hate their jobs. She often says to customers, "It's a great day! How are you doing?" *See how she started the conversation with a positive before she asked the question?* That's a power lead.

Sharon takes time from her work to check in with people. As a result, others now feel she is inspiring. A number of her fellow associates told me they often think: "If she went through all that, and she is being positive, I have no excuse but to be happy today." By starting off each conversation with positivity, Sharon constantly lays the groundwork for cultivating relationships built upon her belief that her choices and mindset defines her experiences with the world—and therefore her happiness. Sharon brings her highest self to each encounter with others. She is a natural-born positive broadcaster, and her kind of power lead takes advantage of the fact that while our brains are sophisticated, they are also limited. We know this thanks to a scientific discovery we don't often talk about, but I want to share it in honor of Sharon.

UNCONSCIOUS CHOICES

Your brain is limited. (Sorry, mine is too!) But that means something extraordinary for the potential of how we can experience the world. In any given second of the day, the human brain can process 40–50 bits of information per second.[7] But while that sounds sophisticated, our brain actually *receives* 11 million bits of information per second. Therefore, it is simply *not* possible to consciously absorb and process all of that. That is why we might taste our cup of coffee while crossing the road and not get hit by a truck, but we might miss our ex sitting outside the coffee shop staring us down. It is simply too much information to process all at once.

That means that each and every one of us is constantly making choices about how we devote our attention. Just like Sharon from Walmart, who woke up each day and chose to either wallow in all of her loss or feel energized by the promise of what the day could bring her, we too have that choice. How are you going to spend those 40 bits? Will you focus on the hassles, complaints, problems, challenges, and ways you feel "less than"? Or will you focus attention on the positive things that are happening, resources at your disposal, strong connections to other people, and ways your life is meaningful?

Choosing to focus on the positive fuels our potential in infinite ways because thoughts that connect us to an optimistic reality engage us with life and make us feel it is worth investing our energy in it. When we focus on the positive parts of our reality, we unlock learning and cognitive resources. Optimism fuels success. But since this book is not just about fueling our own potential, the key is to use this information as a central component of how we influence others.

Being a positive broadcaster starts with refocusing people's attention on the positive before the social script is written. Our natural tendency is to be on the lookout for threats. We are evolutionarily wired this way, and it is thanks to those instincts that we are here today! The skittish caveperson was forced to become an expert at detecting predators—otherwise he'd end up as lunch du jour. These days, life is substantially more stable; our brains do not need to devote themselves to threats in our environment as much. And when it comes to operating effectively in our modern world, science has shown it's better if we don't use a "threat first" system. Because people have limited bandwidth with which to experience the world, when you reorient their brains to positive, they can develop new ways to overcome old and new challenges.

But we all have a friend or work associate who scans their world for the most negative or stressful update and shares it. The key is to get in before they do and set the social script of the conversation to positive and also to realize that *these people are not bad people*. I should know because a few years ago I was one of them!

NEGATIVE PEOPLE ARE NOT BAD PEOPLE

Ugh! I couldn't believe I did it *again*! I had promised myself when I walked into work that night I was not going to complain. I had just about every reason to celebrate life. I had a great job and life in New York City. I had even managed to snag myself a boyfriend. Everything was perfect—except for the one thing that threatened my happiness more than anything: I was constantly exhausted. Exhaustion is my Achilles' heel. My brain falls apart when I am tired, and I become a danger not only to myself but also to others.

I had been working overnights at CBS for the past six months—asleep from 9 A.M. to 5 P.M. (yes, five o'clock in the afternoon!) so I could broadcast during the early morning hours. Dream job; horrible schedule. And I had turned into this horrible ball of complaints at work.

My colleagues would greet me with smiles and warmly ask how I was doing, and my answer was always a variation of the same theme: "I'm tired," "I'm exhausted," "I feel like hell," or something along those lines. That, of course, elicited compassion from them, and the conversation either became a complaint session or ended there. This kept happening until one day I got sick of hearing myself moan. I vowed that even if I just talked about a delicious cup of coffee that night, I was going to say something positive. No more complaining. And what a difference those little words made!

The first night I switched to a positive power lead, I just mentioned how much I was loving my cup of coffee. Yet the conversations with my colleagues went in new directions! On that first night, after such a silly power lead, my producer told me about a house he and his wife were trying to buy. During the second night, I had an amazing conversation with an editor and learned she is an engineer like me. And, as if the universe were trying to prove I was on the right track with this power lead idea, the third night a colleague told me she was so happy to see me in a good mood because she had been wanting to tell me her good news for a while—she was pregnant! My power lead had opened the door for our conversations to unfold in a completely new way—and the proof was in the pudding.

Negative people are not bad people; our brains can just get stuck. We can become really good at finding what's not working and letting everyone know. Even the most optimistic people can find themselves becoming twenty-four-hour, seven-days-a-week very vocal safety inspectors for the world. I devote an entire chapter later in the book to dealing with negative people, but for now here is a snapshot of the three major categories of these negative patterns that we can all fall for.

THE PSA EXPERT

This is someone who cares for you by ruining your day, starting conversations by warning you of all the bad things that could happen to you. The PSA Expert loves forwarding emails and sending worried texts. The PSA Expert tells you about the latest things to be concerned about in life, and usually these cautionary tales are "based on science."

"Did you know that your computer keyboard is dirtier than a public toilet?"

"I heard drinking water from plastic water bottles causes cancer. Which containers do you use?"

"You know what is rampant these days? Feline AIDS." Okay, actually that last one comes from a Debbie Downer sketch on *Saturday Night Live* that I absolutely love. It's a skit about a group of friends at Disneyland who are having fun and talking about the rides they went on, and Debbie Downer keeps injecting PSAs that bring down the energy in the room. It is a hysterical spoof on people who constantly rain on other people's parades.

THE TORNADO

This person starts with their most dramatic experience since they last saw you, and they can turn anything into pure drama. Just like a tornado blows through town leaving destruction in its wake, this person's drama can leave you feeling torn up and mentally drained.

"My boss is ripping the entire company apart, limb by limb."

"All my two-year-old daughter wants to eat is bacon and eggs. She is going to die of malnutrition. How am I going to explain that to the family doctor?"

From their word choices to body language, something big and stressful is going on, and they are going to tell you all about it.

THE SQUASHER

This person feels he or she needs to start with the negative, in a very serious tone, in order to convey the seriousness of the situation, and he or she squashes any hope you may have had of better days ahead. This is a common trap for managers and for parents of rebellious kids alike.

Your boss might say: "The numbers this quarter are abysmal—and the worst is yet to come."

A conference organizer might say: "Welcome to the World Forum. This world is in chaos—politically, financially, environmentally, and we're only halfway through the year."

Your significant other might say: "We need to talk. I don't feel like there is any hope we can make this work." (And they're just talking about the microwave, not your relationship.)

Once you know someone's game, the best approach to use is twofold: Have a compassionate response ready and use the power lead before he or she can dump all over you. Negative people don't need to win. What matters is who speaks first and who is most expressive[8]—even if all you're using are little words.

LITTLE WORDS HAVE BIG MEANINGS

The little words we utter have a big impact on how the conversation unfolds and, depending on the word choice, business outcomes as well. That is all too clear in the results of an experiment done on unsuspecting twenty-year-old college students.[9] What does the following set of words suggest to you?:

Bingo Wrinkle Florida Wise Gray

If you said "elderly" or "retirement," you're smarter than those research participants. Researchers asked half of them to work on a word puzzle with a set of words that were subtle primes of age. The rest of the students were asked to do the same puzzle with neutral words. For part two of the experiment, each student was excused and sent down the hallway to another room. What these students didn't realize was that the second phase of the experiment happened in that hallway.

The students from the "elderly" group were caught on camera walking slightly slower than the participants from the neutral group. Being primed with those little words for just a few minutes had triggered in their brains a response that had made them feel older—and act like it! But we don't want to apply this to the workplace, since we don't want to prime our colleagues to suddenly need walkers. Instead, let's look at the science that connects little words to important business measures.

If you want to build greater team cohesiveness and subsequent success, adding even just one tiny positive word to what you say can make all the difference. In a recent study done at Stanford University, researchers found that including the word *together* had motivated people to work substantially longer and produce better-quality work.[10]

Participants first met in small groups and were split up later to work on challenging puzzles. Half of the students were told that they would be working on them "together" with their peers, even though they would be working on them from different rooms. Each participant would exchange tips with other team members (via the researchers) to help figure out the puzzle. The rest of the participants were not told they were working together with the others; they thought the clues came from the researchers. The fact is that *everyone* was exchanging clues with the researchers.

It is remarkable that those who thought they were working together with the rest of their teammates ended up working 48 percent longer, solved more of the problem sets correctly, and were less tired after the challenge. Just that simple reminder that they were not in it alone had incredible effects. Small words can prime us for substantial shifts in our performance!

Positive priming is central to persuasiveness. If you want to convince others of your ideas, begin with something positive. The power lead puts others at ease and makes them feel more trusting. In a number of studies, researchers would first make participants feel happy or sad and then give them a set of arguments in favor of a given issue. The people who were in a sad mood were less easily swayed overall because they scrutinized the arguments. The positive people, on the other hand, were substantially more likely to be receptive and open to being convinced.[11] This result follows other studies that found that fear caused people to perceive greater risk in their world and to be more risk averse.[12]

The power lead can also be used to unlock untapped knowledge potential. In a study published in the *Journal of Personality and Social Psychology*, researchers primed participants with a positive stereotype ("professor"), a negative stereotype ("soccer hooligans"), a positive trait ("intelligent"), or a negative trait ("stupid"). Those people who were primed with either the "professor" stereotype or the "intelligent" trait did much better on a subsequent general knowledge test, while those primed with "soccer hooligans" and thoughts of stupidity did worse.[13] So ahead of an SAT test, for example, what you say and how you say it can help prepare your child to perform well. At the office, a spirit of optimism at the start of a project will similarly put your colleagues on the path to success.

MAKING IT PRACTICAL

The power lead can instantaneously push the brain into the high-performance zone with just a few words. If you stop for coffee on your way to work, try using a power lead with the barista. In the break room for lunch, share something positive about your life with your colleagues. After returning home from a long day at work, start your evening off with your spouse (the second you walk through the door) with a positive part of your day or ask about something positive that happened in theirs, as opposed to the all-too-common, "I'm exhausted. Today was *quite a day*." Your power lead could even be a quiet kiss with someone you love, followed by a sincere, "I'm so glad to see your face." You never know what might happen if you start off with that!

I'm often told that the power lead is a great idea but that it can be hard to put into practice. So let's talk about all the ways—both big and small—that you can give the power lead a try in your life.

First it is important to identify the areas where you're already great at using the power lead and build upon those. We are all positive in one way or another with some people during some moments of the day. When do you use it and what exactly do you do in that moment? What kinds of things do you say and to whom? Knowing our strengths helps spur our growth.

Now pick one idea from the section below and start building on your current success. Take time to master this new habit; for instance, just add one new power lead to your day for the next twenty-one days at a time when you might have otherwise been neutral or negative. Once that becomes a habit, try adding a second power lead. Eventually, starting your conversations with something positive will become a habit, and it will become easier and easier. But be warned: This whole positivity thing can be addictive! It feels good and might get you a lot of extra attention when people begin to ask what's secretly going on in your life to make you so happy lately!

CONVERSATIONS

Conversations are a great place to begin because we have lots of opportunities to talk to people throughout our day. Scan your world for something relevant that is positive and share it. It's that simple. Perhaps try doing this just once a day initially. When someone asks how you're doing, it's the perfect moment to try out a power lead. Instead of saying, "I'm okay/tired/fine/annoyed at the boss," offer up something good that happened that morning:

"I had an easy commute today."

"I had breakfast with my son, and he was being really funny."

"I'm doing well. My team won this weekend. Super Bowl here we come!"

These kinds of statements tell the person you're talking to that you are in a positive space, and it nudges them to look for something positive to share with you. It is a perfect technique to use with colleagues and clients. What is one positive development you could tell them about? The more people in your life who begin to associate you with an optimistic, I-can-tackle-anything spirit, the better off you are.

One study finds that people who are perceived as optimists are more likeable than their pessimistic counterparts.[14] And in a comprehensive study done by researchers from Stanford and the University of California, Berkeley, employees who both felt and were expressive of their happiness at work received better ratings from their supervisor, higher pay, and ultimately more support from their supervisor and coworkers.[15] They were more attractive to other employees, which led not only to a stronger social support network but also higher levels of overall success at work. Expressing positivity is good for today and can serve as an investment in future success as well because it bonds you more deeply to the people in your life.

My brother-in-law uses the power lead with all of his patients to great result. He is a pediatrician who sees a steady stream of adolescents throughout his day. These teens are going through the challenging years of puberty, braces, and their first awkward dance at the prom. Over the years, he has seen that his first words to his patients each time they come to see him (or even just before a procedure) are crucial. These words either create a connection or destroy it—and that fuels or hinders his success at treating the kids. This is why the first time he meets a new patient he always introduces himself as Dr. Bobo.[16]

Bobo has been my brother-in-law's nickname since he was young, and his family is from Ghana, where you actually find lots of Bobos. But in the United States, Bobo is an unusual nickname, and using it is a great way for him to connect with skeptical or skittish teens. They find it funny. Most kids laugh, which is perfect since it relieves tension and, from a biological perspective, activates the parasympathetic nervous system, allowing their bodies to begin the healing process.[17]

But Bobo's positivity continues from there. He says patient visits go much better when he follows up the power lead by saying something motivational, such as, "You're so brave, you make my job easy!" or "Let's get that shoulder feeling better." We've all heard alternative statements from doctors, including the infamous, "This is going to hurt just a little bit," which Bobo says can cause a child to cry even before anyone touches him.

You don't have to be a doctor or a Bobo to be able to look for a positive opening with people you meet at work. Carefully choose your power lead when you first see your spouse after a day apart. Listen to what you first tell your relatives when you catch up with them after six months. Be intentional about how you answer someone the next time you're asked how you are doing. These are small changes with a big ripple effect.

MEETINGS

Meetings can be life giving or soul draining, depending on your lead. If a meeting leader has positive energy from the start, the time together just seems to flow better, even if some of the topics on the agenda are serious or emotionally challenging. If you lead a meeting, get-together, or conference, begin with positive news, questions, observations, or stories.

Charlie, a manager of quality control at a technology company, was stressed out all the time. Each morning he would receive a list of software bugs that had been reported over the past twenty-four hours. He managed a team of thirty engineers, and his team's job was to fix the bugs . . . fast. When my institute worked with him to develop his positive leadership skills, Charlie told me that he would normally start the morning meeting by focusing on the number and severity of the "fires they needed to put out," in a tone that was anxious and frustrated.

We worked out a plan for the next month. He would try starting these meetings with a power lead of gratitude. At his next meeting, he listed one thing he was grateful for in general, one thing about the team, and one thing about someone specific on the team. And the results were remarkable! He said he still got to all the issues they needed to address during the meeting, but his burst of positivity changed the spirit of the team. He also started to see the average time it took to resolve open items dropped substantially—that is an incredible jump in productivity! He was so convinced of the results of his power-lead experiment that he made this practice a regular part of all of his meetings.

After we shared the research with the executive team at Hugo Boss, the head of the New York office decided to begin meetings with five minutes of positivity. For each meeting, managers would pick a positive topic and have everyone discuss it. For instance, managers would invite everyone in the room to share a story of how a colleague had made his or her job easier. In another meeting, the topic was recent small successes at work that colleagues might not know about. Everyone's brain was encouraged to review his or her workday and come up with something good to share. In the words of one manager, "It's something that takes no more than five minutes but can make an eight-hour difference."

In the classroom, third-grade teacher Ms. Sharon Ketts, from Iowa, found that after she added a positive "morning meeting" to the start of the school day, her students scored higher on all state standardized tests than the three other homerooms and higher than her students from recent years.[18] The morning meetings typically took about fifteen minutes and comprised announcements, news from students, and a fast-paced group activity—typically a game that related to the material they were currently studying.

Research has shown that this power-lead model of the morning meeting helps students to develop cooperation, responsibility, empathy, assertiveness, and self-control.[19] For Ms. Ketts it was the key to unlocking her students' potential. The amazing addendum to the story is that three other third-grade teachers in the school had been trained in the same method, but Ms. Ketts was the only one to actually try it out. She was also the only one to be able to relish in higher scores that year. This is more proof that implementing small changes can make a big difference, but it requires a modicum of effort!

Pastor Joel Osteen uses the power lead to start off services at Lakewood Church in Houston, Texas, the country's largest Protestant church. Each week he tells the congregation that he "always likes to start off with something funny," and then he tells everyone a joke. It's a brilliant way to grab their attention, come together in a moment of levity, and give everyone a chance to settle in to really listen to that week's message. I don't think there is one sermon of his I've heard online that hasn't made me laugh out loud!

In our work, we have also seen success with starting meetings by listing all recent accomplishments or available resources, no matter how small, and concluding the list by reminding everyone that the accomplishments and resources will fuel the goals they are about to turn their attentions toward. Available resources could include new hires or partnerships, existing strategic relationships, or even a new printer in the office—anything that makes success more attainable.

EMAILS

Think about how you typically start off your emails to colleagues and clients. While emails are easy to send, they are one of the greatest causes of miscommunication in the world today. We get all the content with none of the context, such as the sender's tone or facial expression. It is easy to think someone meant something with a haughty tone or a frustrated spirit. If you do not begin your emails with something positive, you run the risk of someone assuming you're coming from a neutral or, even worse, a negative place.

There are an unlimited number of ways to begin an email with positivity. You can do it in the subject line or first line of the message. Most people would always rather open an email with a subject line that reads something like, "Our next GREAT collaboration," versus "Q3 Synopsis Document." Both can be about the document you have to put together with a few of your colleagues, but the second subject line is boring, while the first one is positive and signals a collaborative spirit.

In the body of the email, "Hope you're doing well!" is the simplest power lead to use. Perhaps you could ask about the person's family, hobby, or vacation. The weekends and holidays are a great excuse to infuse positivity into emails; for example, "Hope you had a nice weekend!" or "Hope you're having a great week!" can work well. This tone of positivity is also reinforced when you speak to someone on the phone or in person (which you need to do from time to time to strengthen the relationship).

During a seminar I gave at Philips Healthcare in Orlando, Florida, one attendee there suggested a simple (yet effective) power lead: the word *hi* along with the person's name. He said that some of his colleagues are often so quick to email, they leave off the greeting, and their brief responses seem curt. Consider bringing back simple pleasantries because the extra second it takes to include them in your email could substantially increase your social capital and pay dividends in the future.

I do not advocate being inauthentic at any point, and the frequency of all of these greetings depends in part on the norms for what's professionally appropriate in your workplace. We are talking about breaking away from the pack, but you don't want to stray so far afield that you get a reputation for being "out there" or for wearing rose-colored glasses. That being said, too many people underestimate the power a simple greeting can have to build up storehouses of goodwill between us and other people that we can later draw on should future challenges strike.

REPORTS

Typically, reports don't make the most lighthearted, interesting reading. In order to grab someone's attention, start a report with a positive goal you hope to accomplish with it. For instance, you could begin the document with team accomplishments since the last milestone and where you hope to go from there. These can be small or large goals; the idea is simply to focus readers' attention on the wins to date and the growth potential ahead. A simple line at the top of the report, such as, "Our collective goal is to make our clients enjoy working with us even more by streamlining our accounting system," changes the lens through which someone reads it. It puts the client top of mind and adds a layer of meaning to the project.

POWER-LEAD PARENTING

It's never too early to train your kids' brains to see the positive in life, and using the power lead is the perfect way to do this. When I was in school, my mom never wanted to split carpool duties with other mothers because she said those first few minutes after picking me up were the time when I was most talkative about my day. Everything was still fresh, so I was a chatterbox. And she always asked a version of the same question—"What was the best thing that happened to you today at school?" She trained my brain to scan the world for the good stuff in my elementary school world, even if it was something as simple as having cupcakes for someone's birthday. Similarly, my sister-in-law and her husband regularly begin family dinners with their three girls by expressing gratitudes. They model the behavior of being grateful by sharing three things they are grateful for from their day and then encourage each of their daughters to share as well. The three girls are always so excited to share their lists, and it's thrilling for me to see how their minds work and what makes them happy.

What's the first thing you say to your kids when you see them after school? Power leads can include asking your children, "What was the best part of your day?" or "What was the most interesting thing you learned today?" or "Tell me about a positive experience you had with one of your friends." The questions should lead their brains to scan for something good to share, which reinforces a daily habit of seeing the world through a positive lens.

KICKING OFF YOUR DAY

The power lead is not just for you to use with other people; you can also use it with yourself to put your brain in a good place from the first moment you wake up. Instead of waking up to an annoying buzzer alarm, try using music you love. My friend Kelci has positive affirmations taped to her mirror, and she says them to herself as she brushes her teeth. Another woman I know connects brushing her teeth with counting her gratitudes, and now she counts her gratitudes more than she flosses. And a very successful friend of mine, former FOX News Chicago anchor–turned–investment advisor Byron Harlan, says he always wants to be in a positive headspace at the office, and so he carefully crafted his commute to support that mission. While in his car, even if it is only for ten minutes, he makes sure to play MP3s of motivational business experts sharing wisdom. He says it helps him to fully focus on starting conversations with his clients with a positive lead. While at CBS, my makeup artist, Patrece Williams, always began my day (at 3 A.M.!) with an enthusiastic, warm, funny greeting. I am forever grateful to her for that!

Right before my writing sessions on this book, I would use a power lead and listen to an upbeat, inspirational song to get me in the right headspace. For the past couple of weeks it's been "On Top of the World" by Imagine Dragons, a tune that can put most anyone in a positive mindset! However you choose to start your day, make it good, because it can carry you a long way.

TIME TO EXPERIMENT!

Knowledge is power; putting the science into practice is transformative. We've talked about the effectiveness of the power lead, and now it's time to experiment with it. (As you know, I am a scientist, and I love experiments!) Key takeaways from this chapter are below along with an experiment for you to try out, which will appear at the end of subsequent chapters so you can put what you've learned to the test. These calls-to-action are also great to use with your teams or family members. Get them to experiment with broadcasting happiness and, most importantly, to observe the effect it has on their lives. And I invite you to share the results of your experiments at BroadcastingHappiness.com. Let me know how using the power lead and other strategies in this book have worked for you!

CONCLUSION

Every word we say during our day counts, but especially at the beginning of each new interaction. And we get from this world what we give. If you're already consistently putting positivity out there—that is great! This chapter has been the scientific justification of why your approach is right. If you're not doing it as much as you would like, there is no better moment than right now to boost your signal with a power lead. Scientifically speaking, the best way to get to a good end is to have a good beginning.

((• KEY TAKEAWAYS AND EXPERIMENT •))

THE HEADLINE

The way we start conversations predicts the level of success that follows. Begin with a power lead to set the ensuing social script to positive and raise performance.

THE BIG IDEAS

Start with the Positive

The power lead is a positive, optimistic, inspiring beginning for a conversation or other communication that sets the tone for the ensuing social script. Unlike a traditional negative or sensational lead from newscast, the power lead is a positive headline or story. The power lead motivates teams and fuels others' potential; helps the brain focus on growth-producing areas; spurs others to be positive; and shows that our choices and mindset define our experiences within the world and, therefore, our happiness. The power lead is a technique that anyone, at any job level, can use as a positive broadcaster.

Prime for Success

What we're exposed to first can influence our behavior, which we call "priming." Research shows that priming with positivity leads to better results. We can only process 40–50 bits of the 11 million bits of information we receive each second. Because we are limited in the amount of information we can take in, we must make choices about where to devote our attention. By reorienting people's attention to the fueling parts of reality, we combat the paralyzing effects of negativity and disengagement.

Short-Circuit Negativity

Too often negative people set the social script at work or home. Negative people are not bad people; their brains are just stuck scanning the world for threats in the environment. They need not win; what matters is who speaks first and who is most expressive. Being a positive broadcaster starts with using the power lead to refocus attention on the positive *before* the social script is written.

THE POWER LEAD IN PRACTICE

Conversations

When asked how you're doing, scan your world for something relevant and positive, and then share it. For example, "I had breakfast with my son, and he was being really funny."

Meetings

Begin the discussion with positive news, gratitudes, or stories, such as how a colleague made your job easier.

Emails

Quickly convey a cheerful and positive tone to your email by using an upbeat subject line and beginning it with a simple "Hi" before the recipient's name, followed by something like, "Hope you're doing well."

Reports

Explain the positive goal(s) you're trying to accomplish and focus on the wins to date when beginning a report.

Power-Leading Parenting

Help your children scan for the positive by asking them, "What was the best thing that happened at school today?"

Kicking Off Your Day

Consider doing something good for yourself first thing in the morning, like waking up to music you like instead of your alarm or posting positive affirmations on the mirror.

THE EXPERIMENT

Use the power lead at least once a day for the next week. Perhaps try leading with positivity each time someone asks you how you're doing or start a meeting or dinner with gratitudes. The key is to be consistent and watch the effects that consciously incorporating more positivity into your day has on you and others. After a short time, the power lead will hopefully be second nature and others will come to expect it from you!

SHARE YOUR STORY

I always love to hear the results of your experiments. Please visit BroadcastingHappiness.com to share your story and get special access to additional resources.

FLASH MEMORIES

Leverage Past Wins to Fuel Future Successes

S unnyside High School in Sunnyside, Washington, was not such a sunny place to be back in 2007. The graduation rate was an abysmal 41 percent, an example of what the documentary *Waiting for 'Superman'* termed a "failure factory." And the district-wide student body was so economically disadvantaged that the US Department of Education allocated special grant funding so that *all* the kids at the school received no-cost meals throughout both the school year *and* summer.

But that was not the school I visited in 2014 to address teachers and administrators during their annual school year kick-off event. Sunnyside had transformed itself in seven short years into one of the most-watched districts in the nation. The pride over how far they had come was palpable in the room packed with more than seven hundred educators and administrators. Their graduation rate had more than doubled to 89 percent. How?

The answer was a story repeated over and over by Superintendent Dr. Richard Cole, a story that eventually transformed the entire culture of the school. Dr. Cole made it clear that this was a school of success, not a failure factory. Under his leadership,

Sunnyside received a federal improvement grant, which he used to help teachers institute higher expectations for attendance and stricter off-campus lunch policies, as well as to create constant reminders about grades and other success measures. Following Dr. Cole's lead, the school administrators, teachers, and the wider community became proficient at celebrating what was already working well. They identified stories of success from within the high school student body to share with everyone during assemblies, in newsletters, and on bulletin boards. They gave concrete examples of how the new programs were working to raise grades and engagement, and they highlighted students who were doing well in class or at extracurricular activities. And by inviting everyone (from the superintendent to the gym teacher to the janitor to the bus driver) to greet students each day with enthusiasm and care, together they transformed the school culture from splintered to connected.

The new story of excellence, repeated over and over, became strong belief, not wishful thinking. As a result, the culture conformed to the expectations embedded in the story. For instance, students with a C grade or below in any of their classes were required to spend part of their lunch period in study hall. Those students failing classes went through a mandatory after-school study program. If students were late to or missed class a few times, they had to meet with a guidance counselor to create a plan for attending school. The message to students was as follows: This is an excellent school, so we expect excellence from you because you're worth it.

Ultimately, the key to Sunnyside's success was refocusing on the positive and identifying the ways the school was already successful. It would have been easy for everyone to rehash on a daily basis how dreadful a situation they were in back in 2007. But instead, repeating positive stories became the fuel everyone needed to keep working hard each day. Every time someone doubted that there was potential to raise student grades or improve a very low graduation rate, the educators repeated the examples of success among the school body as proof positive that change was possible.

Let me give a concrete example of this great practice: A few years ago there was a star student who got derailed. Working the graveyard shift to help his family put food on the table, this teenager became exhausted. He could barely keep up with his schoolwork, even though it was clear from all indications that he was a bright kid. And that is when he made a bad decision: to deal cocaine to make some easy money. The police arrested him, and it looked like he was going to be yet one more example of a kid stuck in a cycle of incarceration and disappointment.

Except he wasn't your typical case, and that is what makes his story especially compelling. In the face of these challenges, he made a choice. Working diligently and partnering with some positive mentors at the school, he actually got back on track in a way that was stronger than before. He refocused his attention on his grades, and on the advice of his college guidance counselor, he applied for a Gates Millennium Scholarship, which would not only pay for his college but also any advanced education, such as a master's degree.

Who would suggest to a kid caught dealing drugs to apply for a Gates Millennium Scholarship? I'll tell you: people who believe that positive change is possible at any point. By working hard, identifying the successes that came as a result, and cataloging them in his scholarship application, this young man hoped to communicate to the scholarship committee that he was a worthwhile investment. He and his family were still poor, and it would have been easy for him to slide back into a life of crime. The scholarship would be a golden ticket out of this cycle. And he got it.

The story of this student did not end there. It became enshrined as one of a number of often-repeated success stories at Sunnyside that spotlighted achievements and showed how obtaining success is possible. Note, however, that the stories are not told as the exceptions but rather the rule: "This school produces these kinds of students." There was a constant drumbeat of how everyone's behavior matters: "Where there is adversity, we overcome it. When we are faced with challenges, we persevere and achieve greatness." In the school's recent six-page newsletter, the word *success* was used fourteen times. The school used these themes to shift the student body's mindset away from thinking they were losers to seeing that they were winners and believing that with hard work and tenacity, they were capable of incredible feats.

After the first year of implementing such positive-minded changes, Dr. Cole received the graduation rate numbers. They went up almost nine percentage points. And then that story was used as proof that change was possible. The student body, teachers, administrators, and the community at large listened. And when I took the stage to address the district several years later in 2014, I knew I was preaching to the choir. I was speaking not to a failure factory but to a school with an 89 percent graduation rate (up from 41 percent just seven years prior!). Oh, yes, and with *eight* more Gates Millennium Scholarship recipients.

In this chapter I'll share with you why, in order to achieve success, we need to move our brain past its natural focus on what we need to improve to *what is already working.* We accelerate toward growth when we have perceived progress, not when we feel we still have a long way to go. I'll share with you the science of finding and repeating success stories to fuel motivation and optimism, and how to use these stories to create what I call "flash memories."

A flash memory is the first thought you have in response to a particular stimulus in your environment, and changing it from negative or neutral to positive can dramatically increase motivation and achievement.

In the case of Sunnyside, by changing students' flash memories about their own potential from "I can't" to "success is possible," grades, attendance, and even the graduation rate skyrocketed.

When done right, repeating success stories to solidify strong positive flash memories creates an upward spiral of achievement in the brain as we build upon our previous wins. As a positive broadcaster, you can inspire your children, colleagues, students, and anyone else you come into contact with by consciously repeating success stories—and in turn encouraging positive behavior in the future. Believing that change is possible unlocks our potential and motivates us to take positive action. If you want to lead a team or organization to greatness, the first step is to instill in it a belief that change is possible: Proclaim the dream, look for evidence it is coming, and then celebrate stories of success along the way to the finish line to create optimism, motivation, and results.

NEGATIVITY IN A FLASH

Chicago is an old boys' club, and nowhere is that more evident than at city hall. It was my beat as a reporter, back when I was working in Chicago. Walking down the halls outside the chamber, you can catch bits of hushed conversations among the city's aldermen, high-powered businesspeople, and religious leaders from the Southside's influential churches. During press conferences, if you started asking questions about sensitive topics, the mayor would shut you down. As a reporter, I will never forget the day I realized I was no longer on the outside looking in.

I was there every Tuesday for city council meetings. Fifty aldermen from across the city would convene to battle over some of Chicago's biggest issues. Every Tuesday the same kind Chicago police officer would greet me at the door. Over the course of more than a year, we became friends through conversations about our lives and a healthy Chicago baseball rivalry (go Cubs!).

One day he tipped me off to a big story. There was a secret list. He had heard whispers about it circulating. It was a list of Chicago's roughest officers—the list contained the names of police officers who had more than ten allegations of police brutality against them by citizens. The city and police department were trying to suppress the list in fear they would look soft on internal crime. I knew I had to get my hands on a copy of that list.

I started quietly asking around. The first few aldermen didn't know about this list. As I started running out of trusted people to ask, I found someone who knew where to get it. He told me to meet him in the back hallway behind city hall chambers. The lights were dim when I arrived. I saw him, list in hand, and I remember feeling like this was a scene out of a movie. He handed it to me without a word and disappeared around the corner. It was understood that I was never to reveal my source.

That night on the news, we led with the story of this list that the police department was trying to suppress. The next morning all the other news outlets in town were trying to play catch-up. It was a big win for our team. But it was also a loss—not for us but our community. It was yet another negative blow for the fantastic and hardworking Chicago Police Department. My news story about the secret list of allegations of police brutality further linked them to failure, ignoring their successes. It communicated to citizens that their police department could not be trusted, and it helped strengthen a negative reputation. Many people might hear "police" and think "brutality," instead of a number of other words that could be used to describe the department, including *safety*, *competency*, and *trusted*. Such disproportionate focus on the negative is why we must change the media, but it also points to why we often need to change the way we communicate. Focusing too heavily on the negative creates a negative flash memory.

As mentioned above, a flash memory is the first thought your brain experiences when you think or hear about a person or thing. For instance, what's the first thing that comes to your mind when I ask you about campfires? Do you think of marshmallows? Or do you think about Smokey the Bear warning about the possibility of forest fires? Maybe your first thought is about how, when you were a kid, you got burned while lighting one. Your first thought about a word, person, or topic is your flash memory about it, and it shapes your feelings about that idea.

Let's try a couple more: *House.* Which one did you think of? *Your house.* Was it the outside of your home, something on the inside, or a different house than the one you live in now? *Success.* Did you picture winning a medal or race? Was it a bonus check or bank statement? Was it your kids?

Flash memories directly influence the way we process the world and operate within it. When our flash memories of a person or thing are negative, we steer clear of it. We might feel rushes of panic or anxiety or disgust. Or we might simply feel frozen in place and very pessimistic about someone's or something's potential. A flash memory about a manager, for example, might cause us to disengage with a project not because of the work involved but because negative feelings are associated with the person in charge of reviewing his or her progress on the project.

When our flash memories are neutral, we may not even think twice about the person or thing. It doesn't register in our minds as important. For example, I have neutral flash memories about the Lower East Side of New York, because the few times I visited the neighborhood while living in Manhattan, it didn't make a strong positive or negative impression on me. Therefore, my flash memory doesn't compel me to visit that neighborhood when I am in town, but I also don't feel averse to meeting a friend there if she suggests it.

When our flash memories of someone or something are positive, we are pulled toward that individual or object like an invisible gravitational field. If we have positive flash memories associated with things like our skills, colleagues, friends, and potential for success, our mind is alive with possibilities and positive connections. Many of the students at Sunnyside had developed positive flash memories about school, describing it with words like *high achievement, supportive community,* and *best place to be during the day.* When I was there I asked about their school, and the first things a couple of students said to me were positive, such as, "People here care about us," and "I've heard Sunnyside is fun, and so I am happy to be starting here as a freshman." The students with positive flash memories are the ones who turn toward school instead of away from it.

Creating positive flash memories goes beyond mere free-association thinking. It involves a process that influences the way the brain retrieves the information it has previously stored.

TOTALLY POSITIVE REKALL

"Welcome to Rekall, the company that can turn your dreams into real memories."

In the movie *Total Recall* (the Colin Farrell remake, not the 1990 Schwarzenegger version), a virtual entertainment company, Rekall, promises it can turn your dreams into real memories. Farrell's character, factory worker Douglas Quaid, had been having dreams that he was really a secret agent for the United Federation of Britain. To spice up his life, he visits Rekall to get implanted with a set of memories. He wants to feel like a secret agent, but before he can receive the implant, real agents try to arrest him. I don't want to ruin the movie for you if you haven't seen it, so I'll just tell you that at this point he begins to figure out that someone long ago had altered his memories—causing him to act very differently.

The way we process the world and how we decide to operate within it is largely guided by our memories of the past. Memory recall is the act of accessing information from the past. During each moment of the day, your brain is hard at work encoding your experiences. Your brain's codec—the set of rules it follows to understand and interpret experiences in your life—is based upon the lens you use to process the world around you. When your codec is more optimistic, your memories are encoded with an optimistic spin on them. The opposite goes for having a negative outlook. For instance, if you were feeling particularly negative about a camping trip while you were on it, there is a strong likelihood that you will feel negative about camping in general because of that coded experience in your brain.

During recall, the brain revisits the same pattern of neural activity that originally occurred in response to an event. When we review that retrieved information, we experience an echo of our brain's perception of the original event. In fact, according to neuroscientists, there is no real distinction between the act of remembering and the act of thinking. Both acts retrieve what was previously stored inside the mind.

Much like pages of stored information are found on Google, our brains have stored tons of memories associated with every person we know and every event. In fact, Google is a perfect example, because oftentimes we don't have much time or energy, so if we search for a term online, we usually go right to the very first result in Google. As most of you know, there are thousands of companies whose only specialty is raising your brand's SEO (search engine optimization) ranking. In other words, they're paid to increase a certain URL's ranking in the sequence of results people find when they search for associated terms. That's exactly what Dr. Cole at Sunnyside did; he raised the SEO on the positive so that when people thought about Sunnyside, their flash memories were not about low graduation rates or hopelessness.

What's incredible is that these mental "replays" are not exactly the same as the original "recordings" or encodings, partly because there is an intrinsic awareness that replays are not actually happening in the present. But even more significant is that other information often colors these replays. *If new information is introduced at any point after the original memory was encoded that relates to that memory, it can alter it in our mind, causing us to recall a different version the next time we think about that person, place, thing, or event.* This means that every single memory we have stored in our minds has the potential to be influenced and rewritten. We can shift our own memories, but more importantly, for the purpose of motivating others, we can influence their memories as well.

You can test yourself on flash memories right now to see if there are general patterns present in the way that you perceive the world. Write down your flash memories for the following:

1. Your workplace or school
2. Your past year
3. Your colleagues
4. Your child's math ability (or your own)
5. Challenging people
6. McDonald's
7. Your first job
8. Your country of residence

If you took the time to write these down, and even do a few extra ones, you'll actually be able to observe the lens through which your brain views the world. For some, there are patterns that show up, such as the need for attention or need for power. For others, there is a pall cast over all their flash memories, which is a sign of depression. And for others still, the flash memories reveal a general thread of optimism.

Flash memories are crucial for companies, political campaigns, and marketers because they predict performance. For example, what is your flash memory for McDonald's? Do you think about cheap food or the best quality potatoes in the industry (true fact!) or a lawsuit for a hot coffee spill? What do you think of for Nike—a celebrity athlete or a sweatshop? How about for Walmart? Do you think about how much it pays their associates or how much it donates to charity?

Positive flash memories often don't develop as easily as negative ones. Due to the brain's natural negativity bias—the heightened focus on threats in our environment—we pay more attention to the negative. After a vacation, the memory of the subpar food might stick with us more than the beautiful view we saw from our hotel room. To make positive flash memories stick, it often takes more conscious attention, like Dr. Cole creating a positive flash memory of Gates Millennium Scholarships for students of Sunnyside. It often takes work to build positive impressions about a place or a community and the meaning behind the work being accomplished.

It is possible to rewrite other people's flash memories to shift how they process the current moment. While we might not be able to add in memories like they did in *Total Recall*, we can help mold the ones that our colleagues, students, and children currently hold. For instance, you might have thought elementary school was boring and full of bullies, but after talking with your mom, who provided you with other impressions of the experience, you started to see that you actually had a better time than you thought. You had close friends, liked your homeroom, and had so much fun out on the playground each day after school that your mom had to pry you away when she came to pick you up.

Changing other people's memories by adding in new facts is a process called "creative reimagination," and we make their memories more positive by *repeating success stories*. By repeating positive stories and facts in a way that resonates with others, we introduce new information into the brain. When a person attempts to access that original memory, it will now surface with new data points. Thanks to this new information, the brain will serve up a slightly different memory than before. Introduce enough information that intellectually and emotionally appeals to the recipient, and you can do a massive rewrite of the way they think about a person, situation, or even their own potential for success.

Trial lawyers know this all too well as they "work" with witnesses' memories of crimes and other events. It is possible that they can help create wrongly interpreted memories by simply switching up the words they use. This phenomenon was clearly demonstrated in a study conducted by researcher Elizabeth Loftus, who showed how changing the wording of a question could influence the response.

Study participants were asked to watch a video of two cars getting into an accident and then asked to recall what happened as if they had been eyewitnesses. They were asked specific questions, including "About how fast were the cars going when they (smashed/collided/bumped/hit/contacted) each other?" The speed that participants estimated seemed to be affected by the verb that was used in the question, with those who had been questioned with the word *smashed* reporting car speeds of almost ten miles faster than the group questioned with the word *contacted*.[1]

Ten miles per hour (mph) can make a big difference on the road. (As a brief but interesting aside, it makes such a difference that the New York City Department of Transportation ran an ad campaign focusing on how New Yorkers should drive thirty mph and no faster. Its ad also revealed a shocking fact: "If a pedestrian is hit by a car traveling forty mph or faster, there's a 70 percent chance that a struck pedestrian will be killed. At thirty mph, there's an 80 percent chance that the pedestrian will live!"[2])

Now back to the study and its findings, which indicate our memories about an event are highly malleable. Exposure to new information can modify an original memory. In the realm of potential, this means we can rewrite what the people around us think of their own potential by showing them new information regarding why there is more possibility for them than they currently think. And rewriting flash memories about potential by repeating success stories can have a dramatic impact on a full range of behavioral outcomes.

So how do we rewrite flash memories by using success stories? There are three keys to success: *spotlight the wins*, *select the package*, and *choose the frequency*.

KEY ONE: SPOTLIGHT THE WINS

Almost anyone who has ever looked into buying a home has heard of RE/MAX. Its logo—a hot air balloon—is extremely recognizable, and to many people it is synonymous with the dream of being a homeowner.

For anyone who has ever worked for RE/MAX as a real estate agent, you would have been introduced to their story of "32 Years of Unstoppable Growth." It's the story of incredible financial growth experienced by the company from when it first opened its doors in 1973 until 2004. The story is often told in the form of an awe-inspiring bar graph (which is amazing because bar graphs don't usually have quite that effect on people). This graph, which the senior leaders proudly displayed everywhere they could, shows the amazing positive trajectory of sales spanning three decades—twenty-one million to more than one hundred million—that followed a path much like that of an airplane taking off and eventually morphing into a rocket ship blasting away. The graph is a great sales tool, and it makes you want to work for the company.

But it is not just its financial track record that sets the company apart. It's also the way RE/MAX talks about its work. The company has a philosophy of "doing business that is worth sharing with the world." Set by the core team of top executives, the company exudes a spirit of camaraderie instead of competition by helping one another achieve their sales goals through mentoring, training, and offering continual feedback. Employees always try to stay connected with the meaning behind their work: helping people realize their dream of homeownership. And key executives at the company never doubted that they would be successful. When asked if she was surprised by the company's success, RE/MAX cofounder Gail Liniger said she was not: "In fact, I always thought it should have happened sooner." By shining a light on the successes and the meaning behind their work, the people at RE/MAX fueled even greater success. Just like at Sunnyside High School, focusing on how far they had already come was the key to going even further.

If your aim is to motivate your team, spotlighting current successes puts them in the right mindset for future achievement. Too often I see managers get stuck in the performance trap that causes them to take the opposite approach. They believe that in order to effectively manage their employees, they need to constantly give constructive feedback so team members know what to work on, but multiple studies tell us that's the wrong approach. The same holds true when kids learn a new sport. Their wins should be pointed out at a much higher frequency than the places for improvement.

In a study done with competitive swimmers, researchers found that athletes who received both encouraging and instructional coaching after undesirable performances put forth more effort in the future and were more likely to prefer challenging activities.[3] Additionally, coaches who were quick to praise, offer an abundance of encouragement, and simultaneously deliver instructional feedback were equally motivating to those who were already performing at a high level. Instructional feedback is good, but without an abundance of spotlighting the wins, it can threaten to decrease performance overall.

Our brains are hardwired to scan the world for threats at work, including how we are not living up to expectations. Therefore, as a positive broadcaster, it is crucial to highlight all that is working right. I make the same argument to journalists in the appendix of this book in the Journalist Manifesto, in which I look at how simply featuring positive stories of people who have overcome challenges fuels success in society at large. In business, showcasing the positive can be easily done. For example, PayPal has hung patents on the walls of its offices, as well as a television in the main entryway with a video playing that highlights recent advances from the company. My brother, who is a singer/songwriter and producer in Los Angeles, hung his framed CDs and album artwork on the walls of his studio to remind himself and his team of all their hard work. And while I used to think it was hokey to hang your college degree on the wall of your office, there is major cognitive value in doing that.

Another great example of spotlighting the positive comes from a privately funded investigative journalism body called the Better Government Association (BGA), which could otherwise have only been known for spotlighting the negative. The BGA, headed up by former ABC 7 Chicago reporter Andy Shaw, investigates governmental departments for corruption and promotes reform through civic engagement and by keeping tabs on government officials. But this forward-thinking association didn't want to simply point out the problems and work toward solutions in a lengthy process; it also wants to highlight what is working *right now.*

The Good Government Spotlight was the brainchild of Robert Reed, director of Programming and Investigations. The idea was to offer a chance for members of the community to nominate government employees, programs, agencies, and organizations that "reflect the BGA's core values of government transparency, accountability, efficiency, and fair play for taxpayers and the community." For example, it tells the tale of Chris Kennedy, who, as chairman of the board of the University of Illinois, navigated an admissions scandal that threatened to rip apart the school and brought the school to a new level. The Good Government Spotlight also looked at how, amidst a sea of failing public pension programs, the Illinois Municipal Retirement Fund was able to make things work. The BGA uses its spotlight to showcase how to be successful in the face of challenge so others don't have to reinvent the wheel. Not to mention, it also creates positive flash memories for Chicagoans about their government.

Spotlighting the positive also works wonders at home to motivate your kids. Stuart, a father of four, decided to keep a running list of the funny things his kids would say and do. He had been taking improv and comedy classes for a long time, and he was very excited to see a hearty sense of humor developing in his children, especially the oldest two. Every Friday night at dinner he would share some of the funniest moments with his family, and they would relive them. Often it made everyone laugh and reminded them to look for the funny moments during the week ahead.

Similarly, Zappos CEO Tony Hsieh is known for transforming his company's work environment, turning it into a fun place to work. During a dinner with him, he told my husband and me about some of the ways he helped make the company's call center fun (given that working at a call center can be monotonous). For instance, each work team was asked to come up with a different theme and decorate their workspace to reflect it. When you take the tour of their Vegas offices (yes, they offer tours!), you can clearly see the enthusiasm each team has as its members greet you and show off their artistic creativity and the zeal with which they are helping to revive the economically depressed downtown area. Zappos is intentional about creating positive flash memories for their employees and visitors so that customers not only think about shoes when they think about Zappos, but also about happiness or community engagement.

Which stories can you spotlight to motivate your team or your family? What previous wins have you had as a group? What positive stories can you shine a spotlight on? With your kids, what successes have they had recently? Any examples you have, no matter from how far back or how small they are, can be helpful ammunition.

KEY TWO: SELECT THE PACKAGE

Without personal emotional connection to a success story, it is useless. And often that emotional connection comes as a result of not only the content but also who delivers the message and how. In broadcast journalism, the way you package a story, from the interviews and the visuals you include to how you write it, can have a dramatic impact on how the viewer connects with it.

This was very evident in a clever research study done by fellow positive psychologist and Wharton Business School professor Adam Grant. Grant and his team were looking at how to motivate callers who were raising money for their school, the University of Michigan. As he writes in *Give and Take*, years ago Grant came across a sign in the call center that said, "Doing a good job here is like wetting your pants in a dark suit. You get a warm feeling, but no one else notices."[4]

In order to motivate the callers, at the beginning of the next shift, the staff leader described how the money they raised was used for good, including paying for new construction on campus, top professors, and of course, sports. The impact of this rah-rah speech? Nada. The callers did not raise any more money after that than they normally did.

Grant suggested bringing in a scholarship recipient to talk to a group of randomly selected callers. In just a few minutes, this student explained how the scholarship had changed his life and thanked them for their work. Another group of callers read a letter from him but did not meet him. And the rest of the callers did not meet or hear from him.

During the next thirty days, the callers who had face-to-face time with the scholarship recipient raised an average of 171 percent more money. They also spent more time on the phone overall. Those who had read the letter or had no contact with him showed no change. Hearing the story directly from the person affected by their work motivated the callers in ways the other methods could not. In this particular case, it also gave these callers great stories to share with potential donors, which kept the ripple effect going even further.

The meaning behind the work we do drives our motivation to do more of it and do it well, and hearing from those impacted by our work is an ideal way to share stories of success. Figure out the best way to get someone else involved in sharing success stories with the people you are trying to influence. For instance, you can invite your clients to share with your back-office staff how their work has made a difference. You could ask some former students to videotape a message to their former teachers updating them on how well they are doing so that it fuels those teachers to invest more deeply in their current students. If your child is raising money for charity, perhaps for the kids at St. Jude's Children's Hospital, see if it is possible to take a family trip there so your child can see his or her impact firsthand.

Personal messages are key, and while it is best to have them delivered in person, video can be a great second option. For example, at the opening of its yearly conference, an event at which I was to present, a medical devices company kicked it off with a video of patients whose lives had been saved by doctors using the equipment developed by this company. The video was so well done that the entire room of sales professionals, back-of-fice staff, and distributors were in tears. Videos, not to mention using social media, newsletters, and bulletin boards, can also help reinforce a message the recipient might have first been exposed to in person.

KEY THREE: CHOOSE THE FREQUENCY

Now that you have selected your content and packaged the message in a way that creates emotional connection, the last key ingredient for effectively repeating success stories is—you guessed it!—*repeating* them. Did I mention you're supposed to repeat them? Just in case, I'll say it again—repeat them often.

In his 1885 guide, *Successful Advertising*, Thomas Smith came up with a saying that is still being used today to examine how people respond each time they see an advertisement:

> *The first time people look at any given ad, they don't even see it.*
> *The second time, they don't notice it.*
> *The third time, they are aware that it is there.*
> *The fourth time, they have a fleeting sense that they've seen it somewhere before.*
> *The fifth time, they actually read the ad . . .*

This classic advice (or "ad-vice") still holds true today. Modern-day advertisers focused on getting your attention on their products know that usually people don't even "see" an advertisement the first three times, and it's only by the fifth time that it permeates their conscious brain. If you ever watch TV shows online on streaming sites like Hulu, you know what it is like to be subjected to the same ad over and over and over. (Fine, I'll go buy your stuff, T.J.Maxx!) We don't want to be annoying like Hulu, but we do want to get our message across, and for that repetition is king. Research scientist and longtime head of marketing at the General Electric Company Herbert Krugman found that it takes a minimum of three times for a person to connect to a message. He said we all go through three psychological states in response to exposure: curiosity, recognition, and decision.[5] His research results have become much of what big-time advertisers base their frequency decisions on today.

Repetition is important in order to make it part of a culture, so even if you have told others your positive message, the message here is to tell them *again* . . . and *again*. Oversaturation is rarely the problem. Too often we say something once, maybe twice, and we think the job is done. You might think that other people already know about the positive year-end numbers or the fact that your daughter was named a National Hispanic Scholar, yet in our busy, overstimulated lives, there is small chance the information will be cemented in their minds. The more we say it, the more easily another person will recall it.

Repeating stories at a higher frequency strengthens flash memories. Neuroscientists have found that the information we have previously tucked away inside our brain is scattered in different areas of it, and when we recall a memory, we are pulling from a number of locations. Some describe our organizational system as more like a collage than books on a library shelf, with related information linked together by neural networks and associations. This means as you pull information from your memory, you travel down the same neural pathways created when the memory was first written, and the stronger the pathway, the more quickly you can recall it. Certain parts of the memory might exist along stronger neural pathways, and therefore come to the top of your mind more quickly and easily. This is why you might remember the beer you drank during your last trip to Germany better than where you drank it. The beer was very important to you when you encoded it and you've thought of it a number of times since then. The pub was less meaningful to you. Each time you access information, it is brought from long-term memory into your short-term working memory before being stored back into your long-term memory, thus strengthening it.

A number of studies have shown that thinking more deeply helps create positive associations, and giving people more positive information helps lessen the chances that they will come to negative conclusions.[6] By repeating these positive stories multiple times, we help solidify stronger positive flash memories in other people's minds by strengthening the neural pathways their brains take to get there.

But equally important to repeating the information is how often we actually *test* that knowledge. There have been a number of studies in the field of neuroeducation that show that testing knowledge after learning significantly improves the memory of that knowledge. After a quick "pop quiz," information can be recalled better and faster, with increased overall understanding of the subject and ability to problem solve. It's called the testing effect, and not only does it improve retention for much longer periods of time, it also helps guard against the feeling of being overwhelmed by too much information.

A study published in *Psychological Science* shows that a quick quiz is one of the most effective tools to improve learning. Students scored better on tests that were preceded by frequent pop quizzes as compared to tests that were not accompanied by a prior quiz.[7] (This finding alone motivates me to give my son pop quizzes instead of forcing him to study longer!) Another study found that pop quizzes not only improved performance on subsequent exams, but C-average students were the ones who benefitted the most. They gained nearly an entire letter grade thanks to these surprise tests.[8] Testing not only evaluates learning but can promote it too.[9] Since we want these stories to stick, testing becomes crucial.

At an insurance company, a senior leader we worked with named Larry uses testing during his monthly meetings, except his team members have no idea they are being tested. Each month he asks three people to share a positive story about someone else in the room. In particular, Larry asks each person to describe how a colleague was helpful and made his or her job easier. After each person is done, he asks if anyone else in the room can spot the strengths that enabled this colleague to be so helpful. He is testing them to make sure they listened to the story while also having them identify even more things to praise about the person who is being called out. By simply asking the question and having people answer, the memories of these stories stick with everyone in the room even better.

And I'll say it again: Repetition is the key to creating instantaneous, positive flash memories.

CONCLUSION

We all know that if we don't have a t-shirt for a community event, it can feel as if it never happened. Every time we take that t-shirt for a breast cancer fundraising walk out of our drawer, it is a great reminder of a cause we care about. And without that constant reminder, all the positive work we did that day could easily become a distant memory.

And so it is not too surprising that at Sunnyside High School, you'll often see at least a handful of people each day wearing a black t-shirt with white writing on the back that says, "Empower Each Other. Support. Honor. Succeed." It is the motto they chose during the big transformation from barely getting by to smashing expectations. Students and administrators wear the t-shirt because they've found success. The shirt is literally a black-and-white reminder of it and a great reflection of the sunnier place Sunnyside has become to go to school.

The more we can share success stories to create positive flash memories, the more fuel we have to motivate all of us moving forward. By spotlighting the wins or identifying positive stories, packaging and disseminating the information from the right source to make it personal and emotional, and increasing the repetition of listening and telling these important stories and testing often to ensure stickiness, we raise our chances of creating strong positive neural pathways that can be easily recalled to fuel future success.

((• KEY TAKEAWAYS AND EXPERIMENT •))

THE HEADLINE

Create an upward spiral of success by moving the brain past its natural focus on what we need to improve to what is already working. Leverage these stories of success to create and solidify positive flash memories, which act as evidence that positive change is possible and subsequently fuel motivation.

Flash Memories Shape Our Experiences

A flash memory is the first thought that our brain has in response to a stimulus, and it directly influences the way we process the world and operate within it. A negative flash memory about someone or something typically causes us to steer clear of it, while a positive memory pulls us toward it like a gravitational field. If our flash memories about our potential or success are negative ("failing grades at my school is normal"), motivation and results suffer. Flash memories can be rewritten even years after they were first created.

Rewrite Flash Memories

When recalling a memory, the brain experiences the same pattern of neural activity as when the event happened. If new information that relates to that memory is introduced at any point after the original memory was encoded, it can alter the memory and cause us to recall a different version the next time we think about that person, place, thing, or event. This means that *every memory has the potential to be influenced and rewritten.* You can help people rewrite neutral or negative flash memories into positive ones by adding new facts. This is known as creative reimagination.

The three keys for using success stories to rewrite a flash memory are summarized below.

Spotlight the Wins

If you want to motivate your team, spotlight current successes and put them in the right mindset for future achievement. When we perceive that we've already made progress, we accelerate toward growth.

Select the Package

We cannot simply tell success stories; without a personal emotional connection to a success story, it's useless as a motivator. Emotion can be invoked through the content of the message, who delivers the message, and how it's conveyed. For example, have a client talk directly to your team about how their work has helped him or her.

Choose the Frequency

Oversaturation is rarely the problem. Most of the time, people don't see or hear a message the first time they're exposed to it, which is why repeating our success stories often is key. The more frequently we give people positive information about something in new and different ways, the more we strengthen their positive flash memories and lessen the chances that they'll come to negative conclusions.

THE EXPERIMENT

Identify a situation for which rewriting a negative flash memory could fuel motivation and success. Next, collect positive stories and map out how you will broadcast them to your target audience, using the three keys above. Start broadcasting those stories, test for retention, and notice the effects these new stories have on motivation and perceived likelihood of success.

SHARE YOUR STORY

I always love to hear the results of your experiments. Please visit BroadcastingHappiness.com to share your story and get special access to additional resources.

4

LEADING QUESTIONS

Spark Positive Thinking

Two ten-year-olds hit the streets, cigarettes in hand. They've got people to talk to, and these conversations can't wait. The boy, with his little sidekick in pigtails next to him, walks up to a young woman smoking a cigarette and asks, "Ma'am, can I get a light?"

The woman pauses and looks at the boy a bit confused. "You shouldn't be smoking; it's bad for you."

The duo continues to ask for a light from one smoker after another and gets similar responses from people no more than a decade older than them. None of the smokers would give the children a light.

After receiving a no, the kids would politely hand the smokers a pamphlet and walk away. A camera used by the team from an advertising company captures each smoker reading the following message: "You worry about me but not about yourself. Reminding you of this is the most effective way to help you quit. Call our hotline to quit smoking today." The week after the anti-smoking advertisement made with this footage aired, calls to the hotline jumped by 40 percent.[1]

These children motivated complete strangers to rethink their unhealthy behaviors by using a single question, which was cleverly crafted to elicit the kinds of answers that were much better coming from the smokers themselves than a self-righteous criticizer or even a medical expert. For many of them, the question sparked a mental choice and incited intrinsic (rather than extrinsic) motivation to treat their bodies better. Many of them threw out their cigarette, and no one threw out the brochure.

Too often we focus on the content of our broadcast, and we forget about the power of posing positive questions. Imagine if a middle-aged guy in glasses holding a clipboard came up to the smokers instead and listed out the five most heinous effects of smoking in a dry or heated tone. The smokers would likely have had a negative reaction *and* continued smoking. The same content is entering the mind of the smokers in both cases, but the questions yield better effects. Questions can defuse situations by skirting past a person's mental defenses.

This chapter is about how to use well-timed, well-crafted questions to powerfully change people's stories, habits, and motivations.

It was literally my job to ask questions. As a news reporter, I saw how good questions bring the most important information to light, shift the way people think about an event, and spark renewed interest in a topic. You are taught early on in media training to ask questions that are open-ended, which can lead a person toward the most interesting stories. The same is true in sales.

Jordan Brock, who handles sales and corporate engagements for our positive psychology consulting firm GoodThink, was one of the top salespeople at Dell before joining our company. His sales strategy was simple. Whereas most novice salespeople speak a mile a minute and go through lengthy sales pitches, Jordan would ask a few questions at the beginning of the sales call and then stay quiet for almost the remainder of it. He would really listen to the potential client, and usually that person would make the case for purchasing the product themselves or at least provide a clear solution for Jordan to use. The best salespeople, reporters, therapists, repairpersons, nearly every other type of professional, and even stay-at-home parents benefit from asking questions. Not only does listening to the answers inform your broadcast, it is your key to disrupt negative thinking and make positive messages persuasive.

In this chapter, we'll look at four specific kinds of questions from my media training that I used not only in my interviews with "hostile" guests but also with the most seasoned, polished ones. The goal of these questions is to get the information you need to help inform your broadcast, to switch the frequency from negative to positive, and to encourage the people you're speaking with to start asking more questions—the kind that lead to positive results. As a leader, parent, or friend, employing these questions can give you the information you need to drive the results you want—while getting others to think it was all their idea in the first place.

There are four major types of questions that change the frequency to positive territory and promote positive change: *digging for gold*, *shifting the focus*, *next best*, and *what else*. They can be used individually or in combination to uncover the new story that needs to be told and, similar to our young-smokers example, to change the outcome of your broadcast from resistance to success.

QUESTION TYPE #1: DIGGING FOR GOLD

Asking questions is easy. The real key is asking the right ones. In this section, I describe how to "dig for gold" with your questions, which will help you craft the most effective and persuasive broadcast for change. I love the following story gleaned from the Share

Your Story section of our website (BroadcastingHappiness.com), which perfectly illustrates this type of question.

Francesca, a vice president of sales at a midsize pharmaceutical company, manages nearly three hundred sales professionals from around the country, most of them across great distance. For the annual sales meeting, everyone came together in Phoenix, Arizona. This gathering was Francesca's one chance each year to motivate the entire team face-to-face. In years past, she had delivered long speeches, trying to sell the team on being engaged during the year ahead, based on the company's advances in drug development and patents. She would talk ad nauseam about year-over-year sales figures (read: "boring") to get them to buy into her initiatives for the new year.

One year she decided to try something new—and she struck gold. Ahead of her presentation, she set out to ask different questions, not of the CFO but of the sales reps. She wanted to find out *why* the sales numbers were good. By asking probing "why" questions, she learned that it was not, in fact, just because of the drug patents (for which their competitors had equally good or better ones) or because of their technology platform that allowed them to be highly responsive to clients.

When Francesca asked one of her most successful sales leaders why numbers were up on his team, he told her that it was actually his approach of asking questions and encouraging people on his team to use them as well. Intrigued, because she was asking new questions too, she had him elaborate. He said it was simple: He takes time to connect with clients. He told her that one time a client had to cancel an appointment with him. He had created some social capital with the client beforehand, so he asked if anything was wrong. It turns out the client was not able to meet up because he was undergoing chemotherapy at the local hospital in Columbus, Ohio. The sales rep went to visit the client at the hospital, not to sell him the newest drugs but to comfort him. The sales rep ended up checking in on him often, so much that he got to know the client's family as well. He didn't do it to cement new business, but that is what ended up happening. A combination of compassionate questions and showing up to support the client revealed more information: The client was not only sick but was actually using one of the drugs that the sales rep had been touting. After successful chemotherapy, his client renewed their contract and recommended the company to doctors he had gone to medical school with from hospitals across the country. Good "why" questions had not only led to a sale but became the basis for how this sales leader encouraged his team to approach their clients.

Francesca led with that story in her speech—that sales were up because of the compassion and questions of this sales leader—then followed it up with other examples of dedication, creativity, and ingenuity she heard from the sales team. For example, she described how one rep in California figured out how to save a hospital thousands of dollars on shipping, which resulted in a 5 percent order increase for the next year. By asking the right questions about why success was occurring, her reps told her meaningful and moving stories that she could use in her yearly presentation to the entire team. Afterward, the same reps that used to be obsessed with hitting their targets or too intimidated to talk to her lined up to thank her for sharing those stories or to tell her other ones. She concluded her email to us by saying: No one talked about how sales were up by 22 percent over this time last year—everyone was focused on the meaning behind the work they were doing. That's solid gold.

That was a corporate example, but this method works equally well for parents, teachers, and coaches. So often parents ask the wrong questions as they "interview" their children about their day: What did you get on your spelling test? Did you get your homework done? What time do you have to be at practice? They often miss out on gold with their children. Think about the incredible value you could gain by asking: Why did you get an A on that spelling test? Why did you get your homework done early? Why does the coach make you practice that drill so much? Even asking "What are you doing?" is not very helpful unless you follow up with, "Why are you doing that?" I am not advocating ignoring parental responsibilities by not asking about certain topics. Instead, using these questions can actually help us parent more effectively overall.

My mother-in-law experienced this firsthand one Mother's Day a long time ago. During a Sunday service at church, at the end of the sermon, the children who were at a separate children's service came back into the sanctuary hall carrying the handmade cards they had crafted. Organ music played as the children walked through the white lily–lined hall and handed the cards to their respective mothers. My mother-in-law received my husband's card and, to her initial surprise, saw it was on black paper. Shawn had drawn a large skull and crossbones on the front, a symbol that she had taught him meant poison. Inside it just said, "Happy Mother's Day, Mom." Confused and hurt, tears began to form and she flushed from embarrassment knowing the other moms with their beautiful cards had seen hers. Then she asked Shawn a simple question: Why? He replied matter-of-factly, "Mom, I love you so much I never want you to die." Understanding Shawn's heart, my mother-in-law says that it's still one of her favorite cards to this day. The "why" matters much more than the "what."

What's exciting is that if you're good at delivering "why" questions, you can go from zero to gold in five seconds. Literally. One of the most successful CEOs I know does it almost instantly. She would ask someone, "How are you?" They'd often answer, "I'm good." Depending on their tone, she would follow up with, "Why just good?" or "Why so good?" Done. In five seconds you can go from boring and zero information to the potential for gold. This is one of her easiest strategies that she says has helped her whole career. In order to be a successful positive broadcaster, you need to gather gold first, and asking "why" questions is the key.

QUESTION TYPE #2: SHIFTING THE FOCUS

Another one of the most powerful types of questions you can use is what I call "shifting the focus." The concept is simple: By crafting a question the right way, you ensure the answer goes in the direction you want. In the courtroom, if you have a resistant witness, you can use questions that lead to the answers you want (also called "leading the witness"). Instead of trying to elicit a particular answer, shifting-the-focus questions are used to shift people's thinking or stories away from the negative to the positive.

By asking a well-phrased, well-timed question, you can change the focal point of a person's mental resources, allowing new ideas and patterns to emerge. For example, salespeople use this tactic when they ask, "Do you have the time to spend on waiting for your computer to load?" Well, of course not, I'm a busy person! But the effective salesperson has now shifted the focus away from the cost of a new computer to the cost of lost productivity. Parents also use these types of questions to great effect: "Would you like to go to sleep now or stay up for five minutes and then go to sleep?" I love staying up—I choose that one! But of course the child's brain has refocused on the privilege of getting five more minutes rather than to putting up resistance to the enforced bedtime. By using these questions, you're trying to lead a person—not necessarily toward an immediate guilty verdict or getting to sleep early one night—but toward greater and repeated successes. Shifting-the-focus questions can benefit the person answering them by getting the individual to actively scan the environment for the positive parts of his or her reality. When we want more of the good stuff, focusing on it through our questions is the first step in achieving that.

We witnessed one of the best examples of this technique in July 2010. Burt's Bees is a values-driven personal care products company that prides itself on its mission statement and environmentally friendly initiatives. The company was undergoing enormous change as it began a global expansion into more than a dozen new countries at once. It was growing so fast that some members of the leadership team had never met one another, and with leaders coming from so many parts of the world the company was also dealing with the stress of cultural conflicts in terms of expectations. In this kind of high-pressure situation, many leaders drove people hard toward deadlines and forgot the essentials, such as company values, mission statements, and the meaning behind their work. Employees started valuing productivity over quality of work and quality of life. In doing so, everyone's anxiety level went way up, which activated the portion of the brain that processes threats—the amygdala—and steals resources from the prefrontal cortex, which is responsible for effective problem solving.

Burt's Bees' then-CEO, John Replogle, took a different tack. At the first global leadership meeting, Replogle invited our positive psychology consulting firm, GoodThink, to facilitate a three-hour session with leaders about how to increase happiness at work. By that point he knew our research well and had begun trying it out with the leadership, a practice that especially came in handy when he hit a roadblock during his closed-door, one-hour address on the state of the company he gave to the battle-weary leadership team right before our scheduled training. In the middle of his PowerPoint presentation, filled with numbers and sales goals, he stopped. He looked at the frazzled team and asked, "In the midst of all this growth, when was the last time you had a conversation about the values of our company with your team, and how did you do it?" He then waited until a few leaders described how they had linked the values to their work. Other leaders began to ask the group about the effects that talking about values had on productivity and how to maintain these core values through increased expansion. The cultural differences began dissolving and the stress levels began dissipating as they focused on something more important than deadlines. Their discussion was not a waste of time. Burt's Bees successfully entered nineteen markets within a year, while maintaining its broadcasting of positive values.

In Zen Buddhism there is a paradox called koan, which is a seemingly nonsensical or irrelevant question that is designed to shift the mental patterns of a person's brain. "What is the sound of one hand clapping?" is a famous one. The answer is less important than the question, however, since the question itself gets the person thinking. The meditation student is asked to think for hours (sometimes months!) about how he or she would answer the question. The answer to a koan is seemingly contradictory, but the power is in the thinking. The idea is that if you can shift a person's thought process enough—for example, to abandon one's dependence on reason—it might cause instantaneous enlightenment (as opposed to having to wait decades for its attainment by practicing meditation alone).

One of the best systematized ways to shift the focus in the business world and create some enlightenment right now comes from the research on Appreciative Inquiry (AI), an approach that is good not only for business but for every aspect of your life. In the practical guide *Appreciative Inquiry: A Positive Revolution in Change*, my former professor at UPenn David Cooperrider and his colleague Diana Whitney, founder of the Corporation for Positive Change, wrote the following:

[AI] is about the coevolutionary search for the best in people, their organizations, and the relevant world around them. In its broadest focus, it involves systematic discovery of what gives "life" to a living system when it is most alive, most effective, and most constructively capable in economic, ecological, and human terms. AI involves, in a central way, the art and practice of asking questions that strengthen a system's capacity to apprehend, anticipate, and heighten positive potential. It centrally involves the mobilization of inquiry through the crafting of the "unconditional positive question" often involving hundreds or sometimes thousands of people.[2]

Let's take a look at AI, not in a laboratory but as applied in real life. During the mid-1990s, telecommunications giant GTE (now Verizon) had gone through nonstop challenges, including reorganization, consolidation, acquisition, and then downsizing—and that wasn't the worst of it, as potential new national telecommunications legislation signaled more fluctuations to come. Everyone from senior management to hourly employees was reeling from the upheaval. Without immediate sweeping change, the technology boom threatened to leave GTE in the proverbial dust.

So it was not surprising when an annual opinion and engagement survey that year revealed extremely poor scores for hourly employees, the same ones who served more than 90 percent of GTE's customers. These workers were unhappy with the company, and the toxic conversations at the office reflected their negative mindsets. The senior leaders knew that getting the employees to be positively engaged was the most important key to keeping customers happy (and thus the lights on). The C-suite knew they needed to figure out how to right the ship and right away—or there might not *be* a ship to sail very soon.

Enter researchers Cooperrider and Whitney, who taught leaders at GTE how to use Appreciative Inquiry.[3] The massive course correction started with an endeavor to learn not what was broken at the company but rather "how [the leaders] can engage the positive potential of all 64,000 employees toward the transformation of the company." Cooperrider and Whitney tasked everyone in the company, from the CEO to hourly workers, to continually ask, "What is working well right now that we need to do more of?" Engaging frontline employees in positive inquiry generated a slew of ideas about how to create a flourishing culture at GTE, including initiatives to conduct interviews with customers on exceeding expectations and create measures for service successes, rather than simply focusing on failures, and to begin meetings with positive customer satisfaction stories (which, as you know, is an example of the power lead from chapter two.) But the ripple effect was greater than just the action items that came out of the AI summit.

The act of asking the questions enabled hourly employees to *shift their focus* and change the way they viewed their value to the company, and it gave them a new dialogue at work. Instead of falling back on the addictive habit of looking at all that is wrong at the company, "Appreciative Inquiry provides an alternative 'habit of discourse.'"[4] Not only is this new communication pattern more productive for the organization, it is much better mentally and physically for employees. Positive, action-oriented questions breed positive results.

And as you've seen throughout this book, our communication patterns are predictive of a range of business, educational, and health outcomes. In a recent study conducted by my brilliant friends at the University of Pennsylvania, they have been able to predict levels of heart disease in a community based upon the tweets coming from people living there.[5] By assessing language patterns that reflected strained relationships and negative emotions (especially anger) coming from local Twitter users, the team was able to predict levels of heart disease better than an existing ten-point model that used information such as demographics and health risk factors, including diabetes, hypertension, and obesity. Language expression on Twitter might be a better predictive medical tool than questionnaires given to people at the doctor's office!

Let's get really practical. Here are several examples of shifting-the-focus questions that you can use to greatly improve your broadcast and its ripple effects at home and at work.

"WHEN ARE YOU AT YOUR BEST?"

This was one of the very first questions we answered as part of the master's program in positive psychology at UPenn. I identified the times in my life when I was at my best professionally and personally and the reasons why. Being able to step back and look at those times helped me make small habit changes to take me back there, mentally and emotionally. For instance, I was really happy in Chicago because I enjoyed my job, had a strong network of friends, a robust social life, and exercised most days of the week, specifically taking yoga classes at a studio I loved. I was able to be my best self to others too. I had free time to spend connecting with my friends and could therefore be a good friend to them.

Recognizing the ingredients that comprise our best selves can help us to make small shifts to get back to that optimal state. Ask this question to get others to identify the times when they were at their personal best over any time frame. It will communicate to them that you are interested in what makes them tick and in supporting their well-being. With your team members or your kids, you could also ask, "What did you do to get a good result or grade on that project?" This question helps illuminate the successful parts of the process toward achievement. Breaking down the process into different parts can help someone find the most successful ones and improve or cut out the rest. This way they can best understand where to devote their energies when a similar challenge presents itself in the future.

"WHAT ARE YOUR THREE GREATEST STRENGTHS?"

This is a great question that should be used in every performance review. By focusing on strengths, you activate parts of the brain that record meaning and success. When you then need to talk about the weaker areas, the person can import their strengths to deal with those areas. If you'd like a systematic and well-studied approach to learning your own strengths, I suggest two resources: VIA (ViaCharacter.org) and Gallup's Strengths Finder (StrengthsFinder.com) from my friends Ryan Neimiec and Tom Rath, respectively. Both assessments help you test for your top strengths and provide information about how to use these strengths to increase your success in all areas of life.

"WHAT WAS THE BEST PART OF YOUR DAY?"

Ask this question to get people to shift their focus to the high moments of their day. You can ask them to identify the best part of their entire day, leaving it open for them to choose from all kinds of experiences they might have had over the past twenty-four hours. Your colleague might pull a high moment from her workday, while your daughter's schoolteacher might tell you something personal from her home life. You can also tweak the question to be more specific about the kind of answer you're looking for. You might ask your team, "What was the most productive part of that development process?" Their attention now has a launching point.

One executive we worked with told us how he would ask his two kids at dinner to share their "high/low/funny." They are asked to share something good, something they wish could have been different, and something that is funny about their day, and the stories would bond the family together in laughter. This is a variation of something some parents use called "high-low," and it's one I really like. Some may think that the "low" is not positive, but it is all about how the child and the parent frame it. As long as the child does not gravitate toward or perseverate on the low, then it's important for the parent to gather that intel. Parents could help their children view the lows as local (one part of their larger reality) and temporary.

On Friday nights the executive started his dinner "broadcast" by reminding his kids of funny stories from the week. He also used his stockpile of funny moments on the nights when his kids were not feeling too happy, perhaps because a classmate had been mean. But he wouldn't just seek to distract them; on days like that he would also use shifting-the-focus questions to help them feel better. He might ask his children, "Was anyone at school nice to you today? What did they do or say?" This line of questioning didn't minimize what happened but tried to refocus their attentions on a good part of their school day so they could see that a negative is local, not global.

Shifting-the-focus questions aim to help the person you are talking to rebalance their view of the world. They lead the person back to the parts of life that move them forward and open the door for innovation in the face of challenges.

QUESTION TYPE #3: NEXT BEST

To recap, digging-for-gold questions help you learn information that is beneficial to your broadcast. Shifting-the-focus questions help you move from a temporary negative to something positive. Next-best questions are rarer and usually the last resort: They are to be used when the negative cannot be changed.

In a wing of the Children's Hospital of Philadelphia, Dr. Chris Feudtner manages the care of terminally ill children. With medical advances that allow doctors to prolong a child's life even when there is no chance of cure, new challenges have cropped up, including how long to extend a life when its quality is poor and how to give the child and his or her family the best experience through extremely difficult circumstances.

When it's time to speak with a patient, Dr. Feudtner would ask the child and the parents a very specific question: "Given what your family is up against, what are you hoping for?" Since a cure is unfortunately not an option, this question forces families to look beyond that, to stop wasting mental resources lamenting the lack of a cure, and to begin formulating how to make the best of a bad situation. It's the same approach we can all use when difficult situations arise beyond our control.

Dr. Feudtner says that families usually have a list of seven or eight wishes, including to make happy memories before the end of the child's life, to manage the child's pain well, and to let the child spend the remainder of his or her days at home rather than in the hospital. His simple question opens the door for the pediatric palliative care team and the family to sketch out what their plan will look like and how to make their wishes happen. Together they can move from automatic failure (no cure) to modest success in achieving some of those wishes. In a study published in the *Archives of Pediatrics and Adolescent Medicine*, Dr. Feudtner found that parents who had "more hopeful patterns of thinking" were more likely to choose limits on treatment for the sake of "preventing suffering and promoting comfort, quality of life, and dignity" for their terminally ill child.[6] They influenced the parts of their reality they could control.

Next-best questions move the brain beyond the limits of the current situation to the parts of our reality we can control. These questions can help move a person's line of thoughts from negative to positive and get them to take a realistic assessment of the present moment, while focusing on the parts of reality they can control or change for the better. It helps people break past some long-held assumptions that keep them trying the same solutions over and over, and ushers in new thinking. Next-best questions are provocative, and in business, asking provocative questions is directly connected with innovation. While you don't know the exact destination people will arrive at by answering your questions, asking ones that get them started in a positive direction can improve the final outcome because their answers to these questions will bring forth new information about what is under their control.

Next-best questions open up potential options that were previously hidden. A friend in New Jersey told me how her twelve-year-old son had run away; he was going to take the train to New York City to see his father. She felt like her only options were to close her eyes or go to the train station and force him to come home. My friend was explaining this situation to her colleague at work, who asked her, "What would be the next best option here?" Thanks to that question my friend found another outcome. She decided that instead of letting her son run away or forcing him to come home, she could run away with him. She surprised him on the train and spent the day with him, giving them hours to sort out their issues. That next-best question shifted the way she saw the situation and directly influenced the subsequent action she took.

What would happen if every time you witnessed a gripe session at work, you or someone else asks, "What can we do to create positive change here?" and everyone listened to the answers with a desire to take action? Think how different things would be at your organization if everyone moved from clinging irrationally to rigid patterns of a desired outcome to evaluating new and next best alternatives. Next-best questions direct everyone's mind toward the possible action steps that can create that positive change.

QUESTION TYPE #4: WHAT ELSE?

I'd never met this man before, but that didn't stop him from asking me to sit on his lap and let him strap me to his body.

It was the first in a series of moments in which I needed to let go and trust him ... after all, I was already fourteen thousand feet in the air, and I had agreed to do this.

Over farmlands in Illinois, this virtual stranger and I were going to jump out of a plane with just a parachute (that would hopefully deploy). I had been invited by the US Army Parachute Team, the Golden Knights, to go for an afternoon's skydive for a story for FOX News Chicago. While I instantly said yes when the assignment-desk manager asked me, I regretted my decision just a wee bit the moment I was in the air. The reason is that I like being in control. And in a situation like that, it was very clear I was not.

To make a long story short, the instructor knew I had never jumped out of a plane before and had given me a full training on the ground. Even with this knowledge fresh in my mind, I was nervous. Trying to keep my wits about me as the door to the plane opened into empty air, I asked the one question that had been drilled into me as a journalist: "Is there anything else we missed?" Poised to jump, he paused, thought for a moment, and said, "Just make sure not to straighten your legs at landing. The guy yesterday didn't listen and broke his ankle." I was so glad I asked, because we had *not* covered that before.

We "jumped" (ie, fell like a rock), and after hurtling thousands of feet through the air, my instructor yelled for me to pick my feet up as we came in for a landing and let him handle it. I had to trust him fully. Boy, did I feel the pull to disregard what he told me and do it myself, but I remembered his last-minute advice.

Just like with tandem skydiving, sometimes it is better to let go of control (thinking we know all the answers) and listen for what we forgot to ask. The question "What did I miss?" is perfect because it helps you learn more about things you didn't even know to look for or may not have asked about. You could say, "Is there anything we have forgotten to discuss that you want to add?" or "Is there anything else you want to tell me?" It is too easy to walk into an interview and think you already know the story, but to ask "What else?" is one of the easiest tricks to being a good reporter—and leader. In journalism school you learn to always end interviews with, "Is there anything else you want to tell me that I may not have asked you about?" There have been a number of times when I was surprised by the answers—and those new bits of information actually took the story in a completely different direction.

To ask what else can give your colleagues or kids an open forum to talk about something important to them that you might have missed and can give you surprising information that helps you become more successful. When I was in elementary school, for example, I wrote a short essay on my mom's move to the United States. She was born in Rio de Janeiro, so I asked her all kinds of questions about Brazil and her choice to move to the United States. At the end of the fifteen-minute interview, I asked her, "What else did I forget to ask about?" She told me a great story about her first night in America. It turns out she had arrived in New York City with $100 in her pocket on Halloween and found herself in Times Square, filled with devils, ghouls, and goblins—oh, and she didn't speak more than a few words of English at the time. Imagine that experience! After she told me that story, I started asking a lot more questions and got to know her even better—and my report got an A+.

To ask "What else?" is great for everything from leading team meetings to conducting performance reviews to checking in with your clients or your kids to understanding how to best help your friend who just had a traumatic experience. It's the first question you learn about in journalism school and it's the last question you should nearly always ask at the end of a conversation.

A CULTURE OF QUESTIONS

A single positive question can change the trajectory of someone's thinking or a conversation and dramatically shift success outcomes. But fully realizing the power of positive questions happens when an organization or a family adopts the practice and makes it part of the culture. The key to lasting, sustainable positive change and fostering resilience is getting other people to ask positive questions too.

Certain questions lead to more positive and powerful questions. For example, in Sweden, government officials engage the public to ask and answer important questions facing society. Using so-called study circles, citizens split up into small groups and meet half a dozen times for a few hours at a time. They ask questions about a topic, research a public policy response, and share the information they gathered with officials. This practice encourages people to take a hard look at critical social issues in a way that helps them overcome a knowledge deficit and related feelings of ignorance in the face of complex challenges. When citizens ask the questions, they feel more a part of the process.

Clive, a top executive at a marketing firm in Minneapolis, Minnesota, was very concerned he wouldn't have a company to help run in another year. The boutique marketing firm had lost six of their best clients to a massive national firm that had just opened an office in the Twin Cities. The rumor mill at his company was running rampant with talk of layoffs and people got together in the break room to identify signs of the apocalypse. As Clive nearly pulled out the last hair on his head from the stress he was under, thanks to this aggravating and depressing situation, he had an idea. Instead of trying to figure it out himself, he decided he would engage his team to start asking questions.

The first two most important questions they asked of their former clients were: "What made you decide to switch firms?" and "Is there anything we can do to convince you to come back?" They didn't ask that second question in a desperate way; it was with a practical tone from people dedicated to uncovering the truth and the options for success that come with it. It would put a nice bow on this story if I could tell you that half of those clients realized the knuckleheaded move they had made and returned to the firm, but in truth none of the clients came back that year (though one did two years later). But what did come out of Clive's attempt to shift the story away from stress and fear to education and empowerment was that they better understood the needs of clients in general. His team began talking about ways to secure new clients and, more importantly, better retain their current roster. Questions beget solutions.

From this culture of questions, the team decided to send each of their current clients a custom-made video. In each video, Clive gave a personal and heartfelt thanks to the company for being such a valued client, and then he started to clap. After about five seconds of awkward clapping by one person, the camera panned out to reveal more and more employees of the company clapping, and together they clapped faster and faster. The video ends with a wide shot of the entire company wildly clapping and cheering. It was a message many of their clients told them went straight to their hearts. Not a single additional client left for the fancy new firm. There were no layoffs. The culture of questions Clive's team had asked saved the business.

CONCLUSION

In the past, the news cycle used to be twenty-four hours because newspapers were typically only printed once a day and late at night. The stories that made that night's printer were the same ones that were going to be news the next morning. Now with radio, TV, and the internet, the news cycle is much shorter. Stories can be updated at any moment on social media, and what is important one hour is not even news the next. In business, the news cycle at your company or on your floor at the office can change lightning fast as well. The stories will either motivate people or not. The right questions illuminate important opportunities for change and shift the culture from focusing on debilitating stories to ones that fuel people. Asking questions interrupts current lines of thinking and opens space for an empowering story to emerge. It moves people from deficit thinking to a new conversation. Whether you are the one inquiring or you are getting other people to engage in the practice, questions—along with an openness to fully listen to the answers—elicit new awareness.

Leading questions change the person asking them as well as the person who answers. As we saw with the smokers at the beginning of the chapter, asking for a light can turn on a light in someone's mind.

Let me ask you a parting question: At home and at work, how can you create a culture where questions are continually encouraged and asked in a compassionate way in order to find ways to increase happiness and success?

((• KEY TAKEAWAYS AND EXPERIMENT •))

THE HEADLINE

Too often we focus on the content of our broadcast and forget about the power of posing positive questions. Questions can defuse stressful situations by moving past a person's mental defenses and illuminating new information. We can use well-timed, well-crafted questions to powerfully change people's stories, habits, and motivation.

THE BIG IDEAS

Leading Questions Disrupt
Asking questions and listening to the answers inform your broadcast and disrupt negative thinking, and it's the key to making a positive message persuasive. The goals of good questions are to get the information needed, switch the frequency from negative to positive, and encourage a person to ask more questions that lead to positive results.

Four Types of Leading Questions

- **Digging for gold:** To learn information beneficial to your broadcast, you've got to ask the right questions. Often these are "why" questions that point to the meaning behind the success.

- **Shifting the focus:** These questions help shift people's thinking or stories from negative to positive, getting them to actively scan the environment for the positive parts of their reality. Examples could be asking an employee, "What are you best at?" or asking a spouse or child, "What was the best part of your day?"

- **Next best:** These questions are rarer and usually used as a last resort, when the negative cannot be changed. They move the brain beyond the limits of the current situation to the parts of reality we can control to break past long-held assumptions. Next-best questions are provocative, such as, "What can we do to create positive change here?"

- **What else:** Sometimes it's best to let go of control and listen for what we forgot to ask. By asking someone, "Is there anything we forgot to discuss or you'd like to add?" you might learn about something you may not have asked about and open up new avenues of thinking. To ask what else is great for anything from leading team meetings to checking in with friends. This is the last question you should ask at the end of a conversation.

A Culture of Questions

The right questions move us from deficit thinking, elicit new awareness, and change both the person asking and the person answering. We fully realize the power of positive questions when we get everyone involved in the practice of asking questions and make it part of the culture.

Identify a situation in which a leading question could transform someone else's thinking and accelerate forward progress. Figure out which of the four types of questions might be best in that moment or use a combination of them for maximum success. If you intend to ask the questions yourself, plan out the exact questions you could ask, ideally having at least three in mind. Of course, when you ask the questions, don't forget to listen to the answers. Notice the effect this has on those who are answering.

If you plan to get others to engage in the practice, work with them to get started so they have a positive experience and see the value in becoming more inquisitive. Watch the effects bringing this practice to life with your colleagues or family has on them and group culture.

PART II

Overcome Stress and Negativity

To ignore the negative is irrational. To face it head-on—and help others do the same—with an activated and rationally optimistic mindset creates growth and progress. Positive broadcasters see all parts of their reality but choose to strategically focus on the parts that fuel positive growth.

In Part I, you learned how to leverage a positive mindset to spur success and positive change. But even the most optimistic among us are affected by stress and negativity—so how do we lead others in the face of rampant stress, outspoken negative people, or unavoidable bad news? The strategies and research in the following section address how to rethink stressful thoughts, deal effectively with negative people, and deliver bad news better. Applying these strategies can enable you not only to make it through stressful times but also grow as a result of them—strengthening your signal as a positive broadcaster.

FACT-CHECK

Move from Paralysis to Activation

Joe Stone is a self-described adrenaline junkie, but that passion is what almost killed him. In a paragliding accident, Joe slammed into the ground at sixty-five miles per hour, breaking his back. Yet one year later, Joe competed in an Ironman Triathlon, a promise he had made from his hospital bed soon after doctors told him he would never walk again. While most of us are not as adventurous or as crazy as Joe is, he is an example of a principle so important and rational that it's the topic of this entire chapter.

At twenty-five, Joe moved to Montana to take advantage of all the outdoor extreme sports the state had to offer. One day he went out with a group of friends to do some speed flying, which is a form of high-performance paragliding. On his fifth jump of the day, his parachute didn't deploy correctly, and he quickly realized that there was nothing he could do to stop himself from crashing. He fell straight on his back.

He awoke in the hospital from a coma . . . one month later. The story he was told was a bleak one. Fact: He had broken bones all over his body, including his vertebrae and ribs. Fact: This adventure seeker had become paralyzed from the chest down.

Fact: He was now a quadriplegic because he lost full use of his legs and partial use of his hands to grip things. Fact: Not only would he have to give up his passions, but he couldn't even go for lazy Sunday morning jogs anymore.

Lying in his hospital bed, Joe pictured a life of nursing homes and round-the-clock care. These thoughts were depressing and left him with little motivation to work hard during his physical therapy sessions. And that is where the story could have ended.

That is, until one day something told him that there had to be more to his story. He set out on a new adventure, this time to collect new facts. He started researching to find facts that would fuel him. When doctors told him his body would never function well again, he searched out biographies and examples of other patients like him who had created thriving lives despite their physical conditions. When he feared a life of being a constant burden to the people he loved the most, he actively looked for examples of times when caring for him brought them joy. And when doctors told him he wouldn't walk again, he found facts from medical literature and modern science that showed him a vision of life where he could run—even if it meant it was with the help of a special wheelchair. Just like a skilled journalist, at every turn, Joe fact-checked the story to make sure he had an accurate one.

The new facts he found ignited hope inside him. They propelled him to set a "crazy" goal for a quadriplegic: Joe would compete in an Ironman Triathlon. Not only that, he picked a race that was one day before the one-year anniversary of his accident.

The day he decided to do this, he had no clue how he would swim 2.4 miles, bike for 112 miles, and run a marathon of 26.2 miles—all in one day—but because he was working with a different set of facts than the ones handed to him by the doctors, he believed he could do it. Joe's physical therapy sessions had new meaning. He reached out to wet suit and bike designers to create special equipment for him and learned new things about how the body works and how technology is improving. Each day he learned new facts about his capabilities, and he trained every day he could in order to get in shape for the grueling event.

Instead of approaching the anniversary of his accident with dread, he celebrated it among world-class athletes at the Ironman competition in Florida.

The very first thing any young reporter is taught is not how to look polished on TV or how to be more eloquent. The first thing you are taught is: Check your facts. This is the same process that police officers and Navy SEALs are taught: Check your surroundings, check your assumptions, and check your facts. If you are working from the wrong set of facts, most times your outcomes will be undesirable. Mark Twain put it sardonically, "Get your facts first, then you can distort them as you please."

There is always great room for interpretation and inspiration, but you need the right set of facts to open up the avenues that actually lead to success not delusion. *Fact-checking is the practice of ensuring that you have the right facts to accurately portray the present, but also the process of discovering facts that lead to alternative and more beneficial future outcomes.*

Joe fact-checked his prognosis and the life that he had been handed and found facts that helped fuel him to work hard to create a better future for himself. While he couldn't get his body to transform from paralysis to its former state of health (a delusional outcome supported by none of the facts), he was able to get his brain from paralysis to activation. And now that is what he helps others do. He inspires others through public speaking at schools, showing students how rethinking the present moment can change the future. In the face of everyday challenges, he encourages them to fact-check their stories and get unstuck so they can take positive action to move forward.

In this chapter, I'll show you the way journalists are trained to fact-check and how it can give you incredible power to lead others toward successful outcomes. You'll learn how to fact-check situations that are causing you stress in under a minute. I'll describe the research we have been doing at large organizations like UBS in the middle of a banking crisis to fact-check how the external world affects our health and happiness. You'll learn how to spot the most valuable facts and how to get others to spot them as well.

Very few of my readers will be paraplegic paragliders, but regardless, this principle is for you and may be the most practical one in this book. The next time your child comes home with a bad grade, you'll know which facts best work to move his or her brain away from discouragement so he or she can therefore be more successful next time. When a colleague or friend is stressed out over the same issue for a third or fourth time, you'll know what to say to trigger a shift in their mindset. Likewise, when you feel stuck and deflated, you'll be able to change your thinking patterns so you feel better and don't waste energy stuck in a state of anxiety. The skill of fact-checking builds resilience and positivity in us, and we can use it to change how others experience the world as well. It is a strategy I personally began to practice in the face of one of the most challenging times in my life—a year-long bout with depression—and I have since worked to make fact-checking a habit. Dealt a challenge, my brain starts instantly scanning for facts that show me a more inspiring picture. Positive broadcasters are not only masters at uncovering *fueling facts*—the facts from our reality that give us hope and a feeling of empowerment—they help others do it with ease as well. To introduce this, let me show you why it's important to check the facts about the potential of our brains and bodies—and how doing so can transform our response to adversity.

DOOMSDAY APPROACHES

One week after my husband, Shawn, and I told our entire family we were pregnant, I had a miscarriage. That meant we were going to try to get pregnant again with the infamous deadline looming even closer: I was about to turn thirty-five.

I was concerned what that milestone would mean for my chances of having a baby. All I have heard for years were versions of the same story with the same supposed "facts" repeated over and over. Fact: Your biological clock has a doomsday countdown to thirty-five. Fact: It is substantially harder for women to conceive once they are thirty-five. Fact: The child will probably have developmental problems. Fact: If you wait, your chances of a family or happiness are greatly diminished.

Of course, there were outlier stories here and there of post-apocalyptic success, as well as alternatives available like IVF and adoption, but the doomsday mantra cemented the age of thirty-five squarely in my brain as the cutoff date to youth, attractiveness, and a healthy pregnancy.

Shawn and I were on vacation with some of our friends from Boston, when I saw a magazine headline from across the room, popping out from the stack of magazines on the coffee table. It was "How Long Can You Wait to Have a Baby?" I picked it up expecting the same facts. Instead, I found a positive fact-checker.

The author, Jean Twenge, divorced at thirty, was anxious about how she would meet the right man and have a baby before her body went kaput five years later. She explains that the media coverage of infertility struggles exacerbated the problem:

> My [second] husband and I seemed to face frightening odds against having children. Most books and Web sites I read said that one in three women ages thirty-five to thirty-nine would not get pregnant within a year of

starting to try. The first page of the American Society for Reproductive Medicine's 2003 guide for patients noted that women in their late thirties had a 30 percent chance of remaining childless altogether.[1] The guide also included statistics that I'd seen repeated in many other places: A woman's chance of pregnancy was 20 percent each month at age thirty, dwindling to 5 percent by age forty. Every time I read these statistics, my stomach dropped like a stone, heavy and foreboding. Had I already missed my chance to be a mother?

Twenge's thoughts were my thoughts. Like me, she is a psychology researcher and a natural fact-checker, so she wondered if she had the full set of facts.

In order to investigate, Twenge scoured the scientific literature. Through the simple strategy of fact-checking, she found the following information: The widely cited statistic that one in three women aged thirty-five to thirty-nine years will not become pregnant after a year of trying is based on an article published in 2004 in the journal *Human Reproduction*. However, rarely mentioned is the source of the data: French birth records from 1670 to 1830. The chance of remaining childless—30 percent—was calculated based on historical populations. Twenge writes, "In other words, millions of women are being told when to get pregnant based on statistics from a time before electricity, antibiotics, or fertility treatment. Most people assume these numbers are based on large, well-conducted studies of modern women, but they are not."

I told this fact to a room of seven-hundred fifty women at a conference, and the entire room simultaneously gasped—loudly. Modern research shows a much more encouraging picture for parents trying to get pregnant. As a matter of fact, a 2004 study published in *Obstetrics & Gynecology* found that for women aged thirty-five to thirty-nine years who were having sex at least twice a week, 82 percent of them became pregnant within one year, compared to 86 percent of women aged twenty-seven to thirty-four years.[2] Not only is 82 percent significantly higher than the often-repeated 70 percent, there is only a four-percentage-point difference as we hit our mid-thirties! This study was performed on seven-hundred seventy modern European women. This data, plus a handful of other recent studies, indicates that our thirty-fifth birthday is not, in fact, doomsday after all. (For more mind-blowing data on this subject, I encourage you to read Twenge's article in *The Atlantic*.[3])

Often what we hear in the popular press is different from what you find in top tier academic journal articles. During my master's program I actually took a class that taught us how to read and understand academic journal articles—this is training nearly no journalists will ever receive. Therefore, scientific results are sometimes misinterpreted by reporters or missed altogether. And because it is much easier to Google the latest statistics instead of dig through databases, once a fact, figure, or conclusion gets out there, it often gets play from other outlets that keep repeating it. The system is broken, and unfortunately in this case, it also means that people read scary articles and believe their bodies are broken too.

It was as if a wave of hope and optimism spread over me as I read Twenge's words. What I realized was that, although there are more difficulties getting pregnant as we get older, the picture was not as grim as some make it out to be. Simply fact-checking the story left room for another story to emerge—one of hope in which I had a favorable chance of conceiving. When we believe a hopeful, optimistic story as opposed to a pessimistic one, our behavior shifts as well. (And as I sit here writing these words, my husband and I are the parents of a happy, healthy baby boy named Leo!)

The key to fact-checking a thought or story is to have a realistic assessment of the situation while actively searching for fueling facts. Fueling facts are true parts of our reality that give us hope and a sense of empowerment in the face of a challenge. Sometimes it only takes one optimistic fact to trigger a positive action step; sometimes we need to architect a reality from a number of these facts. They are always out there. These facts do not come as a result of disconnecting from reality. Instead, we identify these facts by consciously shifting to an optimistic lens and using it to reinvestigate our reality.

Bill Gates once opined, "I believe in innovation and that the way you get innovation is you fund research and you learn the basic facts." New directions require a renewed focus on finding the right facts.

FUELING FACTS

Sometimes fact-checking can feel unnatural because it goes against the way the brain is hardwired. Our brains are wired to scan for the threats in our environment and all the problems we need to fix. In psychology this is called the negativity bias. But in most cases this disposition doesn't serve us well. Instead, training the brain to look for facts that fuel a hopeful and optimistic picture of reality can help motivate us. Again, I am not talking about ignoring reality. I'm talking about moving our focus from paralyzing facts to activating ones to create an optimistic, empowered mindset. At a fundraiser, focusing on the money already raised and the outpouring of volunteer support is more fueling than the fundraiser's stretch goal that's been set for the year. Marathon runners who think about their strong muscles or get lost in the music they are listening to have a better experience than the ones who stress about how many miles they still have left. Project managers who are able to see individual team members' strengths or appreciate the available company resources are more successful than those busy worrying about deadlines. Fact-checking to maintain an optimistic mindset in the face of big goals and challenging events or people is what separates the truly successful from the rest of the pack.

As you learned in chapter one, optimism is the belief that good things will happen. Optimistic thinkers believe that negative events are temporary and local (only affecting one domain of life, such as work or a relationship), and, most importantly, they believe that their behavior matters in the face of a challenge. Pessimists believe that negative events are permanent and pervasive and that behavior does not matter in creating a positive outcome. What I always advocate is striving for *rational* optimism, which is taking a realistic assessment of the present moment while maintaining a positive outlook and the belief that if we take positive action, we can triumph over challenging circumstances.

In spite of these definitions, there is a societal myth that says pessimists see reality better. Here are the facts that present a different picture:

- Study after study shows that it is nearly always better to maintain an optimistic mindset because it motivates positive action.[4]
- We are happier, healthier, and more successful when we are optimistic.[5]
- Research shows that when we appraise a situation with an optimistic lens, we are more prone to take steps that lead to success.[6]
- Optimists are more resilient and have a better track record at more quickly and easily overcoming

stressful setbacks.[7] They do better in school.[8] They do better at their jobs.[9] And they make more money over the course of their career.[10]

- Optimists save more money and pay credit card bills more promptly.[11] They are more engaged with life.[12] They form deeper relationships.[13] And they are more likely to remarry after a divorce.[14]
- Optimistic thinking is one of the greatest predictors of success, health, and happiness in life.[15]

So whether you're a stay-at-home parent, a CEO, or a seventh grader, the more optimism you can build into your thinking, the more successful you'll be over the course of your life (and you'll probably have more fun along the way as well).

The author of *The Atlantic* article fact-checked her own story and then broadcasted it for others to benefit. Even more powerful is when we prompt other people to fact-check their own stories. By helping them identify fueling facts in their life, they can start to build a more optimistic picture of the challenges before them. It's like Abraham Lincoln said: "I am a firm believer in the people. If given the truth, they can be depended upon to meet any national crisis. The great point is to bring them the real facts."

THE SCIENCE OF FUELING FACTS AND STRESS

One of the best examples of fact-checking involves Alia Crum, an assistant professor of psychology at Stanford University; Peter Salovey, a social psychologist and the president of Yale University; and Shawn Achor, a Harvard-trained researcher (and, as mentioned earlier, my husband).

As part of the Institute for Applied Positive Research (IAPR), these researchers found that when leaders were asked about the biggest challenges to face them, most of them, regardless of the size of their companies, unequivocally said stress. But instead of doing what everyone else does, which is to figure out how to reduce the stress, this research team decided to check the facts on a story that everyone just assumes is true. They didn't fact-check a stressful situation—they went straight to the source and *fact-checked stress itself.*

What do we hear typically about stress, especially in a stress-management course? Stress is the number one killer in the United States. Ninety percent of all doctor's office visits are for stress-related ailments and complaints. The Occupational Safety and Health Administration (OSHA) declared stress a hazard of the workplace. Stress makes us feel anxious, irritable, unmotivated, and sometimes sad—with physical symptoms including headaches, upset stomach, elevated blood pressure, chest pain, and problems sleeping. Stress kills every major organ in the human body. And what do you feel when you hear this? Stressed!

After a lot of work going through scientific journals, Crum, Salovey, and Achor decided to run a bold experiment with employees at UBS in the middle of the banking crisis. The control group, which included half of the three-hundred eighty total managers, was shown videos about the negative effects of stress and how to fight it. The experimental group with the other half was shown two-minute videos about the enhancing aspects of stress—which are equally valid and often little talked about.

Did you know that from a scientific standpoint, high levels of stress are actually enhancing? It improves your memory, cognitive ability, immune system, and mental agility. Our immune system operates at its highest level during stress. Scientists found that subjects in the midst of a bungee jump can process information much faster than a non–free falling control group. Stress deepens social bonds, which is why the military initiates recruits with a boot camp instead of a beach vacation. Subjects' memories and performances on standard cognitive tests actually increase when they are told to put their hands into ice water—a pretty stressful activity. When a group of patients was purposely made to feel stressed before going into knee surgery, they recovered at twice the rate of a control group not primed with stress. That is why when we are stressed in the right way, we can work faster, harder, and even think better.

The experimental group of managers still experienced the same amount of stress as the control group. However, the group exposed to the equally true but much more fueling facts about stress experienced a 23 percent drop in stress-related symptoms, such as backaches, headaches, and fatigue. Twenty-three percent!

So why do some studies show stress is bad while others show it as good? In their article published in the *Journal of Personality and Social Psychology*, which is one of the top psychology journals, the team from the IAPR proves that what makes a difference is the set of facts about stress a person is using to evaluate his or her situation.[16]

Similarly, the facts you use about work predict the outcomes. The ability to walk others through the art of the fact-check is a signature strength of a positive broadcaster and a strong leader, and the rest of the chapter focuses on helping you develop that skill.

FACT-CHECKING: THE FULL VERSION

Fact-checking can be done in three steps. Let's first look at how we apply it to stories we are struggling with before I show you exactly how to use it to help others. It is best to do this exercise on paper because, just like an algebra problem, it can be hard to work through it all in your head. Oftentimes certain facts can be slippery, and we lose them before they get incorporated into our new thought patterns. Additionally, too often the brain stresses repeatedly about the same kinds of stories, so having a fact-checked story on paper to revisit weeks or months later can save you time and energy. I encourage you to become a master at this skill. And as a positive broadcaster, you can lead other people through fact-checking to help them change their story for the better.

STEP ONE: ISOLATE THE STRESSFUL THOUGHT

Identify the thought that is stressing you out. The key is to identify the simplest thought that is causing problems. For instance, if you're worried about your child, identify the central, current, and most concrete worry it all stems from. You might be worried your child is not going to get into college, but when you identify the real thought behind that feeling, you realize you are actually worried that your middle schooler doesn't like to read. Your child is years away from even applying to college, but his nonexistent passion for reading is signaling to you there is trouble ahead. Those are two totally different situations. If you fact-check the stressful thought that is real, it can simultaneously alleviate the worry about an aggrandized thought.

STEP TWO: LIST THE FACTS YOU KNOW

Find facts from your environment that support the worrisome thought. I know this might sound weird at first—why would we want to find supporting evidence for our worries? This is important for two reasons. First, you want to give yourself a chance to express how you feel and why, which can make you feel as if you've had a chance to vent or "get it out." Second, it gives you an opportunity to understand the experience better. The most important aspect to this exercise is that you only list facts here, not emotions. As you'll see in later examples, to include anything other than facts in this list is counterproductive. So, for the worry over your middle schooler's distaste for reading, facts here could include that he reads only for ten minutes at a time at home, chooses video games over books, and reads only those books he is assigned.

STEP THREE: LIST FUELING FACTS
THAT ILLUMINATE A NEW STORY

This is the "stretch." This part of the exercise is harder because you are scanning your environment for fueling facts that support a completely different story. The key is to find facts that are *equally true* to the facts from the other list, for example, the things that you have not thought about previously.

To return to the example above, fueling facts could include that your middle schooler read a graphic novel about superheroes in one sitting six months ago, his video game prompts players to read on-screen stories to figure out what to do next, and he chooses to read for twenty minutes, three times per week, during study hall during school.

These facts fuel a new picture that not only makes you feel better about your middle schooler's potential but inspires you to take him to the bookstore to let him pick out a couple more of the graphic novels he is excited about. The result: He reads them both in just a few days and excitedly talks to you about the stories.

I invite you to practice this skill with some of your most recurring stresses. Your brain might fight initially against the process of uncovering fueling facts by thinking, "Wait! We already clearly see what is going on here." You need to push past this natural inclination to stick to the story you've been telling yourself all along to find the new, more helpful version of reality. Remember, fact-checking is not about proving yourself wrong; it is about consciously looking for facts that help change or deepen your perspective and move you forward.

Once you are fluent in the art of the fact-check, walking someone else through the process will be a breeze. When guiding someone through the above three steps, there is no need to announce that you're having them fact-check. For each step, you can simply say something like the following:

- **Step one:** *"So tell me what's stressing you out. Boil it down to one or two sentences."* You want the person to keep it simple. If you can get him or her to write it down, it is even better than talking it through, but sometimes asking someone to do that takes social capital you might not have at the moment.

- **Step two:** *"I hear what you're saying. Tell me some of the concrete facts you see that support this picture."* This is the place for facts and not emotions. You might have to explicitly say to this person, "Let's try to focus on the facts and take the emotion out of it," and it might take some guidance from you about what to leave off the list. It is very important not to invalidate his or her story at any point, because that can make that person feel he or she is not being heard or that you are not on their side.

- **Step three:** *"I can understand how you see it that way. I wonder if there is another way we can look at this situation that will help you move forward. How else can we view this situation? What facts might support that point of view?"* If no facts are readily available, brainstorm together. Try your best not to force your ideas on him or her. Give some *possible* ideas on alternative facts and work with him or her to come up with a list that feels right to that person.

The key to success is to be on the lookout for fueling facts. By asking certain questions, you can help someone uncover these facts more easily. The fueling facts will either show that the challenge is temporary or local or that the person has previous wins or current resources to draw on for future success. To help you identify fueling facts and shift your mindset to find true north, use this simple mnemonic device: GPS.

- **Get an accurate time frame:** Help the other person identify exactly how temporary this challenge is or, in other words, how long this challenge could exist. Together, look for past examples in his or her life that show when a similar problem resolved much faster than expected. Get specific about expected timelines and break them up into phases if possible.

- **Pinpoint the smallest domain:** Negative thoughts can start in one area of life, such as at work or in a relationship, and before you know it the negativity has spread to others areas. This happens to me sometimes when I am feeling stressed at work. Without realizing it, I catch myself feeling discouraged about my workouts and contemplating skipping the gym that day. These two domains of life are not related, and yet when one is affected the other can suffer. Find the root domain of a stressful thought or story to help someone take back control and switch his or her mindset back to a more productive place.

- **Scan for available resources and past achievements:**
  A brain that can pinpoint and utilize resources is
  calmer and more prepared to tackle a challenge.
  Help the person you are talking to identify all current
  available resources for use, including relationships,
  connections, help from others, talents, skills, and
  physical resources. Also make a list together of
  previous related wins and achievements, which can
  show the brain that he or she is better prepared for
  the task than originally thought.

Ideally you want other people to generate this list themselves, but often they need a bit of help. That is where you come in: to brainstorm with them fresh ways to see the situation. You can also get them to ask other people for help if you're not the right person for the job.

Let's work through an example that is all too common to see fact-checking in action.

STRESSING ABOUT A DEADLINE

Mark was stressed because his workload kept increasing, and he worried he didn't have enough time to get what he needed to get done. In particular, there was a very important report his boss had asked him to complete ahead of a big presentation the team would deliver next week. Every time he sat down to write, he became overwhelmed, his brain felt cloudy, and all he could think was, "I am never going to finish this project in time."

Eric knew Mark well and could tell right away when his colleague was stressed. He invited Mark to shoot some hoops after work, and after the game Eric asked why he seemed so anxious earlier. Mark said he felt like he couldn't keep up with his work.

So Eric asked, "What in particular are you worried about?" Mark told him about the presentation and how he was worried he wouldn't make his deadline. This is step one of fact-checking: isolate the stressful thought.

Eric decided to help Mark fact-check his thought, "I am never going to finish this project in time," by asking him to tell him why he felt stressed. Mark listed all the following reasons why he felt he would not meet his deadline at work:

- He had a really heavy workload.
- The entire team was busier than they had ever been.
- He had been putting in extra hours lately and felt exhausted.
- His son's recital was the next night, and he couldn't miss it.

It all sounded very reasonable. After hearing out his friend, Eric began to ask Mark questions that would help him uncover some fueling facts. In particular, he focused on the actual wins and resources Mark had available to him that could help him get his report done by the deadline. Eric hoped Mark would see facts from his life that would support a fueling story.

While at first it was hard for Mark to think of anything, eventually he was able to come up with a good list of current resources:

- Three of his colleagues had offered to write sections of the report to take some of the workload off of his plate.
- He had written similar reports before and could use the template as a guide for this one.
- Although his son's recital was the following night and he a couple of family commitments over

the weekend, he calculated that he actually had twenty more work hours to devote to the project. If needed, he could also stay late two nights the following week, bringing the total to approximately twenty-eight hours.

- Generally he was known for working well under the pressure of a deadline. His core skill set included good time management and creativity under the gun.

Mark also listed the following previous wins:

- He had completed a similar report last quarter, and it was well-received.
- He had not missed a deadline in four years, and had only asked for a deadline extension once during the entire time he worked for the company.
- His boss had asked him to be the team lead for this project, despite there being five other people to choose from, because his boss thought him the best person for the job.

Once Mark realized how many resources he had at his disposal, he started to feel more relaxed. Listing these few recent wins also helped him to calm down and feel a boost of positive energy. It enabled his brain to begin to view the project as a challenge instead of a threat, and therefore he could take action steps to leverage the resources and skills at his disposal to get the work done on time.

The next morning, with the conversation with Eric still fresh in his mind, Mark jumped in at work and got more done in one day than he anticipated being able to accomplish the whole week, and he realized he was well on his way to finishing the report ahead of schedule.

Mark's fuel was a list of wins and resources. For Frank in the example below, it was about getting an accurate picture of the time frame and pinpointing the smallest domain.

FEELING LIKE A SLACKER

Frank felt like he was slacking off. He had worked in construction for the past decade and developed a good reputation at his company. He was even promoted last year from a team lead to a project manager, running a number of the company's biggest projects. And yet he felt that he was not giving it his all, and that it would be only a matter of time before everyone found out he was disengaged and didn't deserve the job.

At home he started pulling away from his family. Once a helpful part of the household, he didn't want to do basic chores anymore or even play with the kids. He felt burned out and unmotivated all around.

Frank's wife, Sarah, noticed the change and asked him what was going on. He explained that he felt exhausted by life. Together they identified that the stressful thought he held was, "I am a slacker," and she helped him come up with the following list of facts to support his feelings:

- He was not working as hard as he used to.
- He had been late to work three times in the past two weeks.
- He used to get back to emails right away, but now it took him at least a day or two, and people had noticed his delays.
- He had barely helped out with the chores at home for the past few weeks.

There was no disputing that these facts were true. The question was: Were there other facts that Sarah and Frank could come up with that supported a different, more valuable story? The story that Frank was a slacker was not useful because it ended there. Instead, a new story needed to emerge that would fuel Frank to either get back on track or make a change.

Together, they uncovered very valuable facts that helped Frank get an accurate time frame and pinpoint the smallest domain of life where this stress was originating, namely his work. More importantly, he could see that work itself was not the issue; rather, it was some of the new responsibilities he had been given when he had been promoted to project manager.

This was Frank's new list of valuable facts:

- While he had always enjoyed the work at his company, ever since being promoted, he had become very stressed. The stress occurred when he had to manage the same guys he used to work alongside of. He felt ill prepared, and his anxiety left him exhausted.
- The rest of his responsibilities did not stress him out. He felt very capable.
- Life at home was good. Nothing had changed. The only difference was that Frank was tired from his stressful day and would bring his work issues home. He was also so emotionally spent he no longer felt like helping out around the house.

As a result of this new set of fueling facts, Frank realized he had never received formal managerial training, and Sarah suggested he ask his boss if he could sign up for a seminar or hire a coach to go over some introductory material. The human resources specialist at his company enrolled him in a weekend seminar, and by the following week Frank's anxiety decreased dramatically. His energy level at the office and at home had also skyrocketed.

Often our brains can be tricked into believing that a setback is pervasive, impacting all domains of life. We feel overwhelmed and we mistake those feelings for indications that our problems are everywhere and affecting all things. To fact-check the reach of a challenge can shift our view of it from pervasive to local. With Sarah's help to isolate the challenge down to its smallest affected domain (a specific responsibility at work) and time period (since his promotion), Frank was able to feel more prepared to make small course corrections to solve the issue.

Fact-checking can be used with nearly any stress people encounter. Worried you have too much to do before your vacation and might have to cancel your trip? Fact-check that story and then reprioritize your to-do list to make room for some much-needed time off. Is your child coming home to tell you kids are being mean to him at school? Help your child to fact-check that story by searching together for examples of ways kids have actually been nice to him recently, or help him to identify the number of kids who are bullying him so he can realize that it is only a small group and not the entire class. To fact-check doesn't diminish the seriousness of the bully's actions—it better prepares a child to address the situation with the help of adults because, mentally, your child will feel stronger and in a more supported position.

Is your team at work worried about rumors of layoffs? Have them fact-check that story by looking for ways the company has been good to them in the past and how it has been actually increasing its market share through new products that will help decrease or eliminate the need to lay anyone off. Leaders who are able to successfully refocus attention away from the stressful parts of reality toward the activating ones are those who can fuel success not only in others but also within themselves.

Sometimes you don't have the luxury of time to go through a full, in-depth process to fact-check your story, like in the previous examples. To find true north, all you need is a quick tune-up. By changing just one fact, it is possible to find an entirely new story. We do this by fact-checking quickly, on the go.

A QUICK TUNE-UP: THE FAST VERSION

I'm originally from New York, so I don't really "get" Nascar. Especially on TV. I don't see the fun in watching cars making left turns around a track for hours. To me, the only interesting part of watching a race is getting to see the cars make pit stops. Pit crews are amazing. I have always been fascinated with how fast they can whip around the car, make the necessary tire changes and tune-ups, and then send the driver back out to finish the race. It is a well-oiled machine—pun intended!

You can be the pit crew of fact-checking. When someone else is struggling with a challenge, help the person to get a quick tune-up in thinking so that he or she can get back out on the road to success. If the person is feeling stressed out or sad, walk him or her through this two-minute strategy: Coax the person to tell you what is going on from his or her perspective. Focus on the facts, with as little emotion as possible, to avoid clouding the assessment. Once there is a fact-based assessment of the situation, work together to add, subtract, or reverse a single fact in his or her story.

Short examples for the three tactics are provided below.

TACTIC #1: ADD A FACT

What would the situation look like if we added just one fact?

My Boss Hates Me!

Your colleague is convinced her boss hates her. Every time she interacts with him, she runs to your office to give you three examples of how he is out to get her and is being mean. Their relationship was great during the first year she worked at the company, but for the past six months things have not been the same.

What would her experience be with her boss if she uncovered one additional fact about him? Sometimes knowing one more fact about a person or situation is all it takes to shift someone's perspective.

In this case, you had recently heard from one of your other colleagues that her boss's wife had been battling breast cancer. You tell your colleague that single fact, and her face instantly softens. In that moment she understands why he has not been his normal self during the past few months—he has bigger things going on at home to worry about.

Sometimes the additional fact that changes the story is not readily available, and we need to encourage others to look for it. In this example, if you didn't know what was going on, you could encourage your colleague to ask herself why their relationship or her boss had changed. That might provide the new piece of information that could shift the story.

TACTIC #2: SUBTRACT A FACT

What would the situation look like if we subtracted just one fact?

Headed toward Financial Ruin!

Your husband is worried the two of you won't have enough retirement savings to last until the day you both die. He has two friends who are already running out of money, and they are only in their early seventies. Given your current level of savings, your current combined monthly burn rate, and inflation, he has calculated that you two will have enough money to last until you're eighty-six years old. You both have elder care insurance in the event that a serious medical condition arises, but even with all these resources, he is worried you are both headed toward financial ruin. He pictures the two of you homeless with all your possessions in a shopping cart. Dramatic? Yes. But he believes it is possible.

Ask him what the situation would look like if he subtracted just one thing from his set of facts. For instance, one assumed fact is that you'll always live where you are now. But you've both often talked about relocating to the Southwest, where your son and his family live. That area of the country is substantially less expensive than where you are now. Selling your house and buying something nice there would give you enough capital to last you another seven years. Subtracting the "expensive location" fact shifts the story dramatically and can alleviate the worry that goes with it.

Which one fact could someone drop to change the entire story?

TACTIC #3: REVERSE A FACT

What would the challenge look like if we switched around one fact to an equally true yet completely opposite fact?

Closing In on a Target

Recently I worked with a healthcare company's sales team that fell just short of its sales target. Ahead of the big quarterly meeting, most members of the sales team were worried the CEO would be very unhappy with them and let them have it. They knew they had not accomplished the clear goal set for them twelve months prior. Instead of reaming them, the CEO did something brilliant:

He reversed a major fact. He knew that focusing on the sales numbers one way would kill motivation, while looking at it the other way would fuel it. Instead of saying, "You got ninety-seven percent of the way to your goal but just couldn't pull it off," he congratulated them for closing $291 million of the $300 million in business. He still talked about the fact that they had 3 percent left to meet their goal, but instead of chastising them for not hitting the target, he suggested they tack that 3 percent onto the next quarter's goal because they were so close. It was a very smart tactic to fuel future success, and all he did was reverse the way he looked at one fact.

Sometimes to fuel positive change you need to help someone see an entirely new story. To do that, we can help them fully fact-check with the three steps—and a GPS—to empower them to find the turnaround needed for a new path to follow. Other times a fact-check pit stop is all we need to help others see an experience differently and move forward.

CONCLUSION

The brain can only pay attention to so much of our reality each second of the day. Our power to influence other people comes from the fact that we can easily reroute their attention from debilitating thoughts toward more positive ones by asking them the right questions. Fact-checking the reality before us is an exceptional tool to help someone shift from a pessimistic viewpoint to a fueling, optimistic mindset. And as we have seen from the research, cultivating an optimistic mindset is the key to giving someone the boost he or she needs to have the courage, resilience, and energy to change life for the better. As demonstrated by Joe Stone, the quadriplegic Ironman, focusing on fueling facts inspires forward action and, in turn, success.

Using fact-checking to help people with their problems makes you a better partner, colleague, parent, and friend. Whether you're helping a seventy-year-old retiree who is trying to take care of his family or a young couple concerned about their chances of conceiving, fact-checking can calm their worries and stresses and transform the experience they have with the world.

((• KEY TAKEAWAYS AND EXPERIMENT •))

THE HEADLINE

When faced with a stressful or seemingly hopeless situation, fact-checking the current story to uncover a new set of equally true facts can shift the brain from a paralyzed state to an activated one, spurring positive action.

THE BIG IDEAS

Activating the Brain
It's all too common for our brain to feel stressed by a thought or story, and the result is often poor decision making or feelings of paralysis. If a story is causing us stress, it is imperative to investigate it to make sure it is accurate. The best way to get ourselves or someone else unstuck is to actively question the story we believe in search of a new one that will propel us to take positive action.

Fact-Checking
Fact-checking is the practice of ensuring that you have the right facts to accurately portray the present, but also the process of discovering facts that lead to alternative and more beneficial

future outcomes. What's important is to take a realistic assessment of the situation and spot the most valuable facts—fueling facts, which are the pieces of information from our reality that give us hope and feelings of empowerment. The ability to walk others through the art of fact-checking is a signature strength of a positive broadcaster and a strong leader.

Three Steps to Help Someone Fact-Check a Story

1. **Isolate the stressful thought:** Work to identify the simplest thought that's causing the stress and problems (eg, "So tell me what's stressing you out. Boil it down to one or two sentences").

2. **List the known facts:** Though seemingly contradictory, doing this gives someone a chance to express how he or she feels and why. It allows the person a chance to vent and allows time to understand the experience better. At this stage, be sure to list only facts not emotions (eg, "I hear what you're saying. Tell me some facts you see that support this picture").

3. **List fueling facts that illuminate a new story:** This stage can be challenging because it involves scanning the environment for fueling facts that support a different story. Work to find facts that are equally true and perhaps hadn't been thought of yet (eg, "I can understand how you see it that way. I wonder if there is another way we can look at this situation that will help you to move forward. How else can we view it? What facts might support that point of view?").

A Quick Tune-Up

Sometimes changing just one fact changes the entire story—and sometimes that's all you need. Use a quick tune-up to lift someone's spirit in two minutes.

- **Add a fact:** For example, your coworker thinks that the boss hates her because he's recently been treating her differently. By pointing out that his wife is battling breast cancer, you help your coworker realize that the story is not what she had thought.
- **Subtract a fact:** For example, your husband believes that you're headed toward financial ruin. However, he's assuming that you'll always live where you are now, and you remind him that you've often talked of relocating and downsizing. When the fact that you'll keep your current house is removed from the list of facts, you both can see a new, more positive reality.
- **Reverse a fact:** For example, the sales department fell 3 percent short of its target for the quarter. Instead of focusing on not completing the goal, the CEO congratulates his or her team members on the amazing amount they've already achieved (97 percent), motivating and fueling them toward achieving even more sales in the next quarter.

Characteristics of Fueling Facts—GPS

- **Get an accurate time frame:** Identify how long the challenge will exist. Is it temporary? Look for past examples of similar challenges and examine how long it took to resolve them.

- **Pinpoint the smallest domain:** Negative thoughts can start in one area of life and before we know it, they can spread to other areas. Follow the route to find the source of stress.
- **Scan for possible resources and past achievements:** A brain that can identify and utilize resources is calmer and more prepared to tackle a challenge. Help identify all of the resources available (relationships, connections, help from others, talents, skills, physical resources) and make a list of previous related wins. This helps show someone that he or she is much better prepared than previously thought.

THE EXPERIMENT

First, identify a situation that is causing you stress and fact-check the story. Notice how discovering even just a few fueling facts changes how you feel. Once you're an old pro at how to fact-check your own thoughts, help someone else fact-check his or her story when the situation presents itself. Notice the effect this has on the person's thinking and mood.

SHARE YOUR STORY

I always love to hear the results of your experiments. Please visit BroadcastingHappiness.com to share your story and get special access to additional resources.

STRATEGIC RETREATS

Deal with Negative People

I n November 2014, I received an email from a senior vice president at a tech company who was trying to figure out how to deal with a toxic coworker. Every night she would tell her husband she wanted to quit because of this guy, and she found herself yelling at her husband because of the stress. One day during an hour-long conference call, when this guy had sniped at people throughout the course of the entire meeting, she couldn't stand it anymore. At the end of the call, he asked if anyone had anything else that had not been covered. She blurted out in a caffeine-fueled blast, "Yes, your constant negativity at work." After a shocked inhalation by all the people on the call from Hong Kong to Des Moines, Iowa, he angrily fired back, "Well, I'd be a much happier person if it weren't for other people."

This story says it all. Negative people often feel justified in their negativity and blame other people or the circumstances. Negative people affect our stress levels and ability to choose the positive. We quit, blow up, or die early because of these people. This, in a nutshell, is what we hear from people all around the world. This isn't a corporate or cultural problem; it is a human problem—one that we all have felt.

Once when I was feeling burned out from my overnight job and by some of the frustrating people in my life, I took a vacation by myself to the Caribbean for some R & R (rum and rum). One morning, I purposely selected a secluded part of the beach, laid out a massive beach blanket just for myself, slathered on my lead shield 180-plus SPF on my New York–winter white skin, and stared at the waves. At one point, no one was around me on the beach, no one was walking by, and my brain sighed, "This is heaven." You may have felt this before or wish you could right now, but in that moment it dawned on me that my "heaven" included no souls. There was no one else in my heaven. I had burned myself out on negative interactions and stress so badly, I started to forget that relationships—social connections—are the greatest predictor of happiness. Separating from people leads us away from happiness, most of the time.

There's a great novella by Oxford don C. S. Lewis called *The Great Divorce*, which playfully depicts hell as a "grey town" where people can easily live wherever they want, but because of small disputes, they keep moving farther and farther apart from one another. Some people have moved so far away they never have to see another person again. Think about what that negative guy at the tech company had said—"I'd be happier if it weren't for other people." For Lewis, on the other hand, hell is isolation and complaints, and heaven is relational and vibrant.

As for me, I ended up seeing it as Lewis did, but I needed that momentary departure from the negative people in my life to gain that awareness. I found, after a few days of being away, that I missed some people, even the frustrating ones. I actually felt more compassion for them upon my return (for I had taken a vacation from them, but they had to be with themselves all of the time). A "strategic retreat" from the negative can be crucial to creating positive movement in our relationships at work.

This chapter is one of the most important in this entire book. It is about how you can momentarily shield or separate yourself from negative people without isolating yourself, without cutting negative people off from the world, and without harming your ability to work. Its goal is to assess when you need to use a strategic retreat and how to do it. The key to this concept is that although, yes, there is an initial retreat, it is *strategic*, meaning it allows you to retreat, regroup, and reenter the fray stronger than you were before you left it. As Sun Tzu writes in *The Art of War*, "Victorious warriors win first then go to war; defeated warriors go to war first then seek to win."

In this chapter you'll learn how to identify when to make a strategic retreat from a negative person or conversation, how to regroup and refortify your resources, and how to best plan a reentry that fuels positive communication and deeper connection (or at least doesn't have you wishing you could hurl yourself off of a building). No matter whom you encounter, this chapter will help you deal more effectively with negative people so that not only are they no longer able to shift your mindset into negative territory but you are also able to have a positive effect on them.

THE STORM SPREADS

"How do I deal with a negative person in my life?" This is by far the most common question I get when speaking at various companies. Although it is asked often in terms of dealing with a negative person on a team at work, there are some in the room who may be thinking about how to handle negativity from a spouse or in-law. Think about the senior vice president who blew up on the conference call at the beginning of this chapter—if we don't figure out how to deal with negative people, it harms our mental well-being and causes undue stress. So, strategic retreats are also about protecting our own ability to choose happiness.

One time I spoke at a women-only event in Southern California and a petite blonde woman cornered me in the bathroom afterward to ask about how to better handle her husband. She explained, "I am the optimistic one in the marriage, while my husband is the pessimist, and it's killing me." I could hear the concern and frustration in this woman's voice, and even a touch of desperation as she tried so hard to help him "see the light." She kept butting her head against a wall every day for years, and she was at the breaking point. I've been there. And I have definitely encountered my fair share of thoroughly negative people affecting my own mood and performance. I'm willing to bet you have a person in your life like the one I'm about to describe in this story.

It was my first day at work. I'd been hired as a news reporter for the noon and 5 P.M. broadcasts in El Paso, Texas, and my assignment was a drug bust. While El Paso is the seventh safest city in the country, thanks to a massive federal law enforcement presence, including the DEA, CIA, and FBI, its proximity to the US–Mexican border means drug raids are common. When it comes to news stories, drug busts are about as easy as it gets. As long as you stick to the "who, what, when, where, and how" of the story, you should have no problem. That is, unless you're nervous because it's your first day on live television in a new city, and you're paired up with Negative Norm the Sh*t Storm.

From the moment we got into the news van on my first day of work at KTSM El Paso NewsChannel 9, the spewing began. My cameraman's lead was, "So how the hell did you end up in Hell Paso?" He listened to half of my answer before blasting the driver in front of us and complaining about the traffic on I-10. He offered to give me a "tour" of local joints as we drove past them on the way to the story. He pointed out every place I should *avoid* because they "suck." It seemed like every restaurant in the city was either rat infested, received a C grade from inspectors, or simply did not know how to make a decent burrito. By the time we arrived at the press conference, I was seriously rethinking my decision to move there.

After the song and dance at the DEA office, we parked in front of the drug den. Norm set up the camera, and at 11:55 A.M. he handed me the microphone. We did an audio and video check with the producer back at the station, and we were all ready to go—when I heard Negative Norm starting to have one of his "storms." A button on the camera was not working, and he got very upset. I stood there trying to run through my notes and practice what I was about to say on TV, while his tirade became louder and louder. His complaints about the busted camera button transitioned to "crappy equipment" and "not supported here," and then there was no turning back. It was a Category 5 storm.

And his monsoon rained all over me. During the live shot he was huffing and puffing in the background. It was very distracting for someone trying to be coherent on live TV. Not only did his behavior ruin his day, it sure put a tsunami-sized damper on mine. He jammed my brain, and I tripped over my words and had to correct myself twice on air during my report.

Yes, happiness is an individual choice, but almost every choice is influenced by the people around us. Don't underestimate the harsh effects negativity can have on our bodies and performance. The negativity discussed in this chapter can take many forms, including gossip, criticism, and disinterest, and most types are detrimental. Repeated exposure to negative people can cause anxiety, which can lead to physical symptoms, such as headaches and exhaustion. Negative people have the ability to impact us down to a cellular level, and repeated exposure to life's stresses could potentially even shorten our life span by destroying the

DNA telomeres at the end of our chromosomes.[1] Put another way, Negative Norms shorten your life.

To make things worse, negative emotions emitted by others are highly contagious.[2] In seconds, they can rain their negative energy all over us. It is even more contagious if they are highly expressive of their feelings.[3] We are wired to be empathetic to other people, and thus we often absorb their emotions. Stress and negativity even spread when the source doesn't say a word. Our brains can pick up on nonverbal cues and micro facial expressions that then shape the way we interpret the world.[4]

A study conducted at the University of Georgia found that negative thoughts are so contagious that depression can actually spread from person to person.[5] Exposure can move us from feeling optimistic to feeling anxious, annoyed, or deflated. Negativity pulls the mind away from the parts of life that make it worth living and refocuses our attention on things that can worry us or make us feel separate from other people. If we are not conscious of the negativity around us, it is too easy to become like a sponge, absorbing other people's toxicity.

I have worked with many executives, at companies around the world, who struggle with negativity on their teams. However, I've found that the biggest problem a manager usually has is just one person. One. One Negative Norm or Petty Patty. A manager from Samsung in Korea told me, of the time he spends managing his people (versus projects), he ends up devoting about 40 percent of it to one particular tech lead on his team. The employee is both highly negative and highly expressive. The manager invests a huge amount of time either talking directly with that employee or cleaning up the messes he creates with team members and clients. When a negative person like that spreads toxicity to others at work, it lowers the productivity of nearly everyone around him. And in today's economy, with Gallup estimating that more than 65 percent of workers in the United States are either "not engaged" or "actively disengaged," the effects of negativity at the office is costing companies collectively more than $500 billion in lost revenue each year.[6] Is Negative Norm worth $500 billion?

Sometimes moving negative people to another department or letting them go is an option and may be the best solution for everyone. I worked with a senior director from Google's New York City office who is passionate about supporting the personal and professional interests of her team members. Try as hard as she might, there was one dark cloud on her team that she couldn't get to change his ways. He was chronically negative and tearing apart the rest of the team. After nearly two years, the director finally gave him the option to transfer departments. At first she felt bad: She could be dumping her "problem" on someone else. But this particular story has a happy ending, since the employee changed departments and actually flourished. It was a win-win situation. However, the stars don't often align like that; it is more likely we need to figure out what to do with the cards we've been dealt.

Since negative people can have such deleterious effects on us, we need to be battle ready. You wouldn't show up to the battlefield in your bathing suit. Instead, you would wear all the gear you need, mentally prepare yourself, and make sure the location and environment works in your favor. The same goes for encounters with a negative person. We do this in three steps: (1) strategically retreating, (2) regrouping and refortifying our resources, and (3) creating a reentry plan—or for short: *retreat*, *regroup*, and *reenter*.

RETREAT

Often the most effective way to deepen conversation is to retreat from it. A strategic retreat is when you recognize that communication is hampered and the battlefield is unfavorable, and thus you need to consciously pull back from the conversation to give yourself and that person a time-out so that you'll connect in a better way when you return.

I have managed our company's website over the years, and I have had to call in to tech support a number of times. There have been instances when someone would take the call and seem to have no idea what I'm talking about. (Granted, sometimes I have no idea what I am talking about either, but still . . .) I've found that there are moments when the best way to get some real help is to politely say thank you, hang up the phone, and call back to reach someone else who *does* know what I'm talking about.

A retreat is a powerful move, even though the word is often thought of negatively in relation to battles. If you back down from the enemy you could be considered weak or uncommitted. History, though, tells another story. Wars have been won thanks to the use of strategic retreats. George Washington commanded his army to strategically retreat a number of times during the American Revolutionary War, which helped to guarantee the survival of the Continental Army. On August 27, 1776, at the Battle of Long Island, the British defeated the American troops, and Washington had them flee to safety at a fort nearby. Later that month, under cover of dense fog, Washington led another retreat of thousands of men to Manhattan by boat, only a few months later to retreat again to a fortified position in upstate New York—followed by another location high in the hills. Finally, in 1777, near Philadelphia, when the British advanced from behind, Washington himself led a fight that held them off and allowed most of his soldiers to make it to safety.

Sometimes conversations with negative people are losing battles for us. When we are confronted with a losing situation, we need to accept defeat in that moment in a way that allows us success in the future. A strategic retreat enables us to preserve our resources (both mental and physical) and create the space to formulate an action plan for the future.

There are three criteria to assessing when a strategic retreat from communication can actually enable better communication in the future. If you or the conversation matches any (or all) of the following criteria, it's time to pack your bags and walk.

CRITERIA #1: YOUR DEFENSES ARE DOWN

You are not on your A-game. Your brain is foggy or you feel stressed. Perhaps you are tired or haven't eaten for a while. Check in with yourself to make sure you're not in a challenged headspace, because that can hamper your abilities to think clearly when dealing with a negative person. If you don't, you might be more impulsive or reactive, as opposed to letting your calm, collected self guide the discussion.

There is a great acronym from addiction recovery programs that can help you take an inventory of your defenses: HALT—which stands for hungry, angry, lonely, or tired. It is a self-care tool to help you check in on your emotional and physical state. You can use it to assess if you're in the right place to engage with a negative person. If you are H, A, L, or T and you do engage, it is much easier for the conversation to spiral downward. Sometimes it is best to hold off or retreat in these moments.

As for me, I have learned not to call one of my more antagonistic friends when I feel tired because I just end up annoyed, or I say something to her that I later regret. Assessing your own mind and body can tell you if your defenses are down.

CRITERIA #2: THEY ARE DEEPLY ENTRENCHED

Sometimes the person you're talking to is too emotionally charged to listen to or even be around you. It's a bad time to be exposed to this person or attempt to have a conversation. Being sensitive to their level of emotional arousal is the key, because if they are fired up, you might end up getting hurt—emotionally or even physically. Take a temperature reading, and if it's too high, it's time to step away. Just like you learned as a child not to ask your mom for candy when she was mad, you shouldn't try having an important conversation with someone in a fired-up negative state.

CRITERIA #3: YOU ARE OUTNUMBERED
OR SURROUNDED

There are situations when it is simply the wrong time or place to discuss something with that person, when talking about a certain topic would go against the accepted social script for that moment. Just like you don't want to be talking about your spring-break trip at a funeral, you need to choose the right moments to engage with negative people.

A couple of years ago, I worked with an executive at a financial firm in Boston who told me that when it came time to meet for a performance review with one particularly negative person on his team, he scheduled it for the end of the day. That way, the employee could go home right afterward and not infect anyone with her postreview frustrations (because she was sure to have many).

Along with wrong place, wrong time, sometimes the audience is not ideal either. Depending on who is in the room at the time, highly negative people can act completely differently.

I know a young couple that tries to visit their parents together because both sets of parents are better behaved that way. If either of them visits his or her parents alone, they forget the niceties reserved for non-blood-related people, and they let loose with trash-talking and insults. Adding or subtracting one or more people from a conversation with a negative person can transform it. Ask yourself if the social makeup of the group will hamper communication.

Any time you encounter something that matches one or more of the above criteria, it is time to take a step back. You can use it at the office, but the strategic retreat is also ideal for improving relationships with people at home. Eleanor, a client of mine, wanted to improve her relationship with her husband. They were having more arguments than usual, and she wanted to figure out what to do to help the situation. Overall, her marriage was very good, but these arguments were taking a toll on their happiness.

Together we came up with a description of a typical argument, including the who, what, when, and where of it. We found the common theme was that most of the arguments happened during the first hour after her husband came home from work, and that most of them were about topics they would not normally fight about at other times. As a matter of fact, most of them were relatively silly fights.

Eleanor crafted a plan. She decided to use the strategic retreat with her husband during that first hour after work on days when he seemed to be feeling very frustrated. If he had a stressful day at work, she would give him time to cool off before trying to discuss anything significant with him instead of ambushing him right after he walked through the door. Eleanor became an expert at quickly picking up the signs that her husband was stressed and strategically retreating. And when she returned, the flow of their conversations was much different. It was such a simple tweak, but it created an entirely different trajectory for their evenings and their relationship overall.

Sometimes after retreat, reentry is not as easy as it was for Eleanor. There are certain interactions with people that leave us drained and wishing never to see them again. It is not always possible to escape for a rejuvenating beach vacation to the Caribbean. There are times when we need ways to effectively prepare for reentry in the midst of real life, and we do that by buffering our brain and regrouping.

REGROUP

At this point in the book, it is important to note that you will continually be frustrated by the negative if you are not practicing positive habits to buffer against it. Positive habits are simple, quick behavioral changes you can make to your life to increase your levels of positivity and reduce stress in just minutes. Your first line of defense against a negative person is to put at least one of these positive habits into practice. Think of this as preventative medicine.

When I was working overnight at CBS News, I had downtime between 11 P.M. and 1 A.M. I'd eat my "lunch" and sometimes watch a show on TV. As you can guess, there isn't much on at that hour, so I got to be the reigning expert on infomercials. They all promise one of three things: better health, better wealth, or a better butt.

I always watched infomercials with skepticism, wondering if their newfangled inventions really worked. So when I started researching at the University of Pennsylvania during my master's program, I wanted to know the science behind what really works when it comes to creating and sustaining a positive mindset. Is it possible to actually shift our mindset from negative to positive in minutes, or would promising this simply be material for another false infomercial?

It thrills me that, after more than a decade of research, we have been able to isolate certain positive habits that create a more positive mindset and buffer our brains against the effects of stress. For those of us who are busy with an active life full of work, family, and a million responsibilities, the best news is that these routines take just a minute or two each day. (And you won't need a butt exercise machine to do them.)

We featured the following three positive habits during the "The Happiness Advantage" special on PBS and, as we told viewers, we encourage you to *pick one of these habits and do it every day for a period of twenty-one days*. The research shows that doing something for twenty-one consecutive days helps us to build a life habit. These habits will help inoculate your brain against stress and negativity from the outside world by shifting the lens through which you view your life to a more positive one.

SEND A POSITIVE EMAIL

How to do it: Every day for twenty-one days, first thing in the morning, send a short positive email of praise or thanks to someone you know. The goal is to draft the email in two minutes or less. Recipients can include colleagues, your spouse, a childhood friend, or even someone you don't know too well, such as the security guard at the front desk of your office. If you don't have their email address, consider a quick handwritten note. The key is to tell these people at least one way in which they have made a positive difference in your life.

Why it works: Sometimes it feels as though thinking about a negative person consumes our mental resources. Our brain churns as we consider the ill effects this person is having on us and how we are going to handle future encounters. We also often forget about all the life-giving people we have in our lives. This exercise, in just minutes each day, reminds our brain of our deep social-support network and puts into perspective the size of the role that the negative person actually plays in our life. Social support is one of the greatest predictors of happiness. And every time we meaningfully connect with one of our email recipients, we shrink the level of influence the negative person has on our life. That space becomes filled with positive, soul-nourishing people who only make our lives better.

COLLECT YOUR GRATITUDES

How to do it: Every day, for twenty-one days, write down three new and unique things you are grateful for in life. Make sure to be specific and to briefly explain why you are grateful for them. For instance, you might write that you are grateful today because your son told you he loves you, which made you feel very special. It is important to come up with new items each day so that at the end of the three weeks, you have more than sixty-three documented gratitudes.

Why it works: Actively cataloging the things you are grateful for in life trains your brain to scan the world in a more positive way. Instead of scanning for things to complain or be stressed about, your brain starts to *first* focus on the parts of your life that are positive and meaningful. In just one to two minutes a day, you can build new neural pathways in your brain for higher levels of positivity. In a study conducted at Eastern Washington University, researchers found that listing three gratitudes for just one week not only produced a significant boost in feelings of well-being while engaging in the practice, but also it continued to climb for participants weeks after the practice ended.[7] In a similar study—this one conducted with a group of people aged sixty and older—researchers found that a two-week gratitude practice led to a significant rise in well-being that held steady even a month after participants had stopped counting their gratitudes.[8] Engaging in the quick daily habit had lasting effects on their happiness.

SNAP A POSITIVE PICTURE

How to do it: Every day for twenty-one days, take at least one picture of a meaningful moment or thing in your life—a sunset, your child sleeping, a project at work you successfully finished, or perhaps the meal your spouse cooked that night. Make sure to capture a moment in which you felt positive emotions, such as happiness, gratitude, joy, peace, serenity, or love. At the end of each week, scroll through the pictures you took to remind yourself of the emotional highlights of the week.

Why it works: Photos can trigger emotions in just seconds, even decades after they were taken. The positive pictures you take remind you of the emotions you felt while taking them, and by reviewing them, you effectively relive those times, doubling the amount of positive emotions you felt as a result. Additionally, the practice of taking photos of positive subjects on a regular basis trains your brain to watch for moments to capture. Similar to the effect that counting your gratitudes can have on your mindset, positive pictures can cause you to feel more optimistic as you literally begin to adjust your viewpoint of the world.

It may seem like these easy little habits are too simple to spark big changes in your mindset and energy levels, but we've read about the positive effects in the thousands of stories we've received from people. Doing one of these positive habits (or more if you feel so inclined) refocuses your attention on the positive and meaningful parts of your day, which, by default, ends up shrinking the power negative people have over your mindset; they lose their ability to strongly influence how you experience the world. The simple act of practicing gratitude or scanning the world for the positive shifts the focus away from stress and negativity, not to mention it gives us the unique energy boost that comes from remembering the best moments from our life and the positive emotions we experienced during them.

REENTER

In *The Art of War*, Sun Tzu says that a good general will always pick the time and location of battle. If you give these up or neglect to think about them, you are inviting disaster. The same is true if you want to turn the tide of battle at home or work toward the positive. Now that you've strategically retreated and fortified your resources by regrouping using the above positive habits, it is time to craft a reentry plan. It takes attention to make a plan, but it is energy well-spent when it helps you neutralize the negative person's power. Reenter a conversation more effectively by knowing the terrain, bringing reinforcements, and practicing your two-minute drill.

KNOW THE TERRAIN

The first thing you need to do is get to know the potential battlegrounds. This includes the place, time, and duration of your reentry into the space with the negative person. There is no science to this, because every person and moment in time is different, and with each person there are a number of potential battlegrounds. (That's why it's called *The Art of War* and not *The Science of War*.) But there are some general patterns you can look for. Try to capture the high ground. Make sure you find a time when that person is likely to be less busy and less stressed and in a (relatively) good mood. It's easier to keep the conversation positive if you're beginning closer to positive in the first place. This seems obvious, but you have no idea how many managers, in my experience, try to reengage with a person right when they are most fired up (remember criteria #2!). And be sure to do it in a place where you have the advantage, if it is at all possible to craft your location. Engaging with this person in the hallway with others around might be a better idea than going into an office and shutting the door. As often as possible, find the time and place that will facilitate a productive conversation and lower one's ability to unleash negativity. It is also important to figure out beforehand the best duration of the encounter. I always like to keep it short and sweet, though this is not always possible. There have been times when I have been paired up with a negative cameraman and stuck in the news van with him all day. Try to find the best length of time, and make sure to stick to it, even if you are enticed to stay longer because things are going well. One of my close friends has twice extended trips to visit her "challenging" parents because they were getting along well, and twice she has called me saying she regretted her decision. Get in, accomplish the mission, and get out unscathed.

BRING REINFORCEMENTS

In battle, soldiers bring reinforcements to raise their chances of success. The same goes here, though the reinforcements in your case won't be a squadron of Boeing AH-64 Apache helicopters. Your reinforcements will be other positive people who can help disarm the negative person. Either actively bring a colleague, friend, or human resources manager with you for the next planned encounter or just make sure that unless other people are around, you won't engage in more than a polite exchange of greetings.

Reinforcements diminish the strength of the negative person's signal because there are more positive people present to counterbalance it. A marketing specialist once told me she had the absolute best conversation with her terrible boss at the holiday party when her husband was present—so much so, her husband told her afterward he didn't believe all the stories about her "awful" boss she had told him over the years. Her husband's energy had diffused the boss's toxicity. (Though, to this day, she is not sure if the reinforcements were her husband and the other guests—or the cocktails being served at the party!)

PRACTICE YOUR TWO-MINUTE DRILL

College and professional sports teams repeatedly practice running the "two-minute drill"—and this is a brilliant strategy to apply when crafting your reentry plan. In football, teams often get the ball when they are down and with only a few minutes left on the clock, so they script out exactly which plays they are going to run so they don't have to waste time trying to coach one another on the fly. They know the play calls, they know where they are supposed to run, and they know which passes have the highest success rate and take the least amount of time. When I reengage with a negative person, I always have my two-minute drill. I know the three topics that are going to be safe and help me gain ground, and that I can do quickly to get to the goal I want. When I was on that beach vacation, I planned out a couple two-minute drills I would use when I first saw one of the negative guys back at my office—depending on the location I ran into him. I practiced for different defenses. I practiced if he tried to blitz me. So when it came time, I was much more prepared for those two minutes than the negative person was.

I received this example "playbook" from an accountant at a technology company in California. He typically needs answers to quick questions from his negative colleague and has to visit his office to get them because he doesn't respond quickly to email. The accountant's aim is to get in, get the information, and get out before being sucked into his colleague's negative vortex. His two-minute drill is simple but effective.

Two-Minute Drill: Operation Get Quick Answer

1. **Power lead:** I will knock on the door of his office with a smile. When he acknowledges me, I'll step in but not sit down. I'll say, "Congrats on the finished project." I know he just got praised for finishing a project that went really smoothly so I plan to open with that. In case he badmouths the leader (because he has done that before), I have prepared a positive response: "Well, at least he gave credit where credit is due. You knocked it out of the park."

2. **Complete the mission:** I plan to ask him the question I need an answer to, making sure to keep it simple. I'll listen to his answer and keep any follow-up questions to a minimum.

3. **Leave on a good note:** I will thank and compliment

him: "Thank you for this information. That was
really helpful. I am thankful you have such deep
knowledge about this subject. It makes these
projects go much more smoothly to know we have
the information we need. Thanks!" I plan to walk
out of his office right away.

The accountant told me that the drill went flawlessly on his
first try and he has used it with slight variations a number of
times since, to much success. Whether you've been going to
battle lately with the office manager or your mother-in-law, practicing a two-minute drill can be incredibly valuable in getting
the information needed or communicating the necessary message without getting entrenched in toxicity. Strategic retreats,
regroups, and reentries are empowering and diffuse other people's negativity. They also have the potential to change the way
you think about another person—to see them in a different light.
Or, like Charlene, a teller at a bank in Florida, a strategic retreat
might even bring you love.

Charlene noticed that each week the same man would come
in to make a deposit. He was hard to miss. He seemed miser-
able, and he was often rude to the bank employees and other
customers. Every time he stepped up to her window he snarled,
said something snappy, and complained about the long line, the
deposit slip, or something else.

While having coffee with a friend, Charlene explained her
feelings of dread each time he walked in. To her surprise, her
friend suggested silently sending him thoughts of love. At first
Charlene thought this was crazy talk, but her friend convinced
her to try it out. She told her to make it a game. The next few
times the grumpy man walked through the door, Charlene was
to think, "I love you." That was her silent two-minute drill.

Of course, Charlene felt very silly for a while there. She thought, "I love you. I love you. I love you." He never responded. Yet she stuck with her drill no matter how foolish it felt, and then after about two months, something changed. He looked up at her and smiled. She smiled back. The following visit, he told her he needed help managing his books, and she offered to give him a hand. She eventually came to find out that he was unhappy and angry because he had lost his wife, and while the grief was passing, it was a hard process. Her thoughts of care for him grew so much so that, two years later, they got married. You never know what even a silent strategic retreat will bring your way.

CONCLUSION

Just as negative people can influence our brain, so too can we influence them. After all, this is what much of this book is about. And because the highway of emotional contagion goes both ways, every time you have a positive encounter with a Negative Norm or a Petty Patty, you are shifting their reality. Each time you don't sit with them in their toxicity or play misery poker to see who has the best hand, you elevate them above their current line of thinking. As Sun Tzu wrote in *The Art of War*, "The supreme art of war is to subdue the enemy without fighting." The goal is how to turn negative people positive without losing your own battles—or even fighting in the first place. By being more strategic about your encounters with negative people, you can save your energy for activities and relationships that fuel your success and happiness (and if you do find yourself needing a strategic retreat beach vacation, give me a call!).

((• KEY TAKEAWAYS AND EXPERIMENT •))

THE HEADLINE

Negative people are a human problem, not just a corporate or cultural one, and dealing with them can be challenging. It is possible to improve communication with negative people by making a strategic retreat so that they are unable to shift your mindset into negative territory and, conversely, you are able to have a positive effect on them.

THE BIG IDEAS

Negative People, Dire Consequences
Negative people can increase our stress and hamper our ability to choose the positive. It is important to protect ourselves against negativity because it can have harsh effects on our bodies, leading to headaches, exhaustion, anxiety, and shortened life span. Negativity in the workplace can dramatically lower productivity and engagement. And since social support—having strong, healthy relationships—is the greatest predictor of happiness, challenging relationships with negative people can detract from our sense of connectedness to others.

Retreat, Not Defeat
A retreat may be cowardly, but a strategic retreat is courageous and can help create conditions for a better relationship later on. Strategic retreats have long been used to win battles. In this sense, you can use it to defeat the ill effects of someone else's

toxicity. A strategic retreat allows you the chance to regroup and reenter the fray stronger than ever.

Retreat

Sometimes the most effective way to deepen a conversation is to retreat from it. It's time for a strategic retreat when you find the following:

- **Your defenses are down:** Your brain is foggy and you're feeling stressed. If you're HALT (hungry, angry, lonely, or tired), realize that these states hamper your ability to think clearly when dealing with a negative person and may lead you to become more impulsive or reactive.
- **They're deeply entrenched:** If they're too emotionally charged to listen or to be around, it's time to step back.
- **You're outnumbered or surrounded:** It simply might be the wrong time or place or the timing might go against the social script of the situation. Don't engage if it will fuel more negativity.

Regroup

You'll continually be frustrated by negative people if you're not practicing positive habits (quick behavioral changes you can make in your life to increase your levels of positivity and reduce stress) to buffer against the negative.

Daily positive habits can include sending an email of praise or thanks, writing down three new and specific things you're grateful for in life, and snapping a positive picture of something that makes you happy, grateful, joyful, peaceful, or loved and reviewing the highlights at the end of the week. Practicing these habits refocuses your attention on the positive and meaningful parts of your life.

Reenter

A good general picks the time and location of battle. When reentering, do the following:

- **Know the terrain:** Logistics include the place, time, and duration. Try to find a time when the other person is less stressed and busy and in a relatively good mood. Do it in a place where you feel you have the advantage and stick to the amount of time you have scheduled.
- **Bring reinforcements:** You raise the chances of success when you have other positive people who can help disarm the negative person. Together you diminish the negative person's signal because there are more positive people to counterbalance it.
- **Practice your two-minute drill:** Just like a sports team plans its moves, practice your plan by visualizing different defenses, and prepare yourself for any locations you could run into this person.

THE EXPERIMENT

Every time you have a positive encounter with a negative person, you're shifting his or her reality. Identify a relationship you have with a negative person that might benefit from a strategic retreat. Make sure to regroup and craft a reentry plan following the guidelines above. Notice the effects that using this strategy has on subsequent interactions with the person and if you were able to successfully lessen the hold he or she has on your happiness.

SHARE YOUR STORY

I always love to hear the results of your experiments. Please visit BroadcastingHappiness.com to share your story and get special access to additional resources.

THE FOUR Cs

Deliver Bad News Better

C an you imagine getting a speeding ticket and being happy
afterward?

Being a police officer means many things, and one of
those certainties is that people will file complaints about you.
From frustrated speeders who are sure the radar guns are not
calibrated correctly to irate stop-sign rollers who feel that the
cops should focus on "real" criminals, complaints are part of
the territory. Typically these grievances are not egregious, just
people upset, rightfully or wrongly, after their encounter with
an officer.

At one precinct in Los Angeles the same holds true—unless
you're Sheriff's Deputy Elton Simmons. While every single one
of his fellow officers received at least a couple of complaints, last
year he received zero. The year before was also zero. Let's save
some time: During the past twenty years—after making more
than twenty-five thousand traffic stops—*he has not received a single
complaint*. Rumor has it that he was even invited to dinner after
one of his traffic stops.

Officer Simmons is a master at delivering bad news better.
As a traffic cop, his job is to deliver bad news multiple times

an hour every workday of the year. And yet, after more than two decades, someone has never felt angered enough to find fault in his approach. Moreover, people applaud his style. From the tone of his voice to his careful word choice to his studied nonverbal behavior, Simmons goes off script. He does not act like one of those self-righteous or indifferent cops from the movies; instead he shows empathy and is able to tell you what you don't want to hear in a way that makes it palatable. He is able to encourage better behavior and make you want to be a better person.

Simmons follows the four Cs of how to scientifically deliver bad news better. He does the following:

1. Creates social *capital* by looking the person in the eye with a friendly, warm expression on his face, and speaks in a soft tone of voice, using plain English instead of cop-speak.

2. Gives *context* to the situation. Instead of merely explaining the violation and the fine, he talks to people about how, together, they can keep the community safe and how road safety is better for the families that live there.

3. Expresses *compassion* for the fact that a driver made a bad choice with its resulting negative consequences. His words and tone of voice communicate sincerity, and people seem to realize he is not nasty, trying to make his monthly ticket quota, but rather he is giving them the benefit of the doubt.

4. Stays *committed* by giving drivers not only his advice about what to do to remedy a certain situation, but also his contact information at work in case they have any additional questions. Nearly

no one takes him up on the offer, unless of course
they want to invite him for dinner.

Simmons delivers the same message that many of his fellow
officers do, but the way he delivers it not only makes him unique,
it makes a huge difference in how it is received by others.

After one of my talks, a manager came up to me and said,
"Thank you. I'm only going to say positive things from now
on. I'm not going to see anyone's weaknesses; I'm going to only
compliment people. I'm just going to try to be really happy and
positive all the time." The woman meant it as praise for my talk,
but I realized if that was her takeaway, I had failed to fully do
my job.

Bad news is part of life; ignoring it—"*ostrich*cizing" ourselves
(see chapter one)—means that we never make this world a better
place. We have to address the things that need fixing in our kids'
behavior or in our performance reviews or in our society. But
how you deliver bad news is what makes the difference.

In this chapter, we will explore how you can talk about the
negative without sounding or becoming negative. I will walk
you through the four Cs in multiple domains of life from work
to home to relationships. Whether you're giving someone negative feedback on a project, conducting a performance review,
responding to a crisis at your company, telling a client the ship-
ment won't make it there in time, or letting your mom know
you won't be home for Thanksgiving this year, I'll show you the
science behind how to make these conversations produce better
outcomes. In most cases, mastering this skill will enhance your
charisma with others and also allow you to sleep better at night
when hard times strike. Not only will you be viewed more favorably and create positive change, but you'll also be able to draw
on the social capital you created before and during the process
toward future success.

STEP ONE: CREATE SOCIAL CAPITAL

Scott was excited to start his new job in management. Scott, who says his wife calls him "ruthlessly practical," evaluated the team he was inheriting. It was clear that there were two people he needed to let go in order to run the team well. As he was telling me this story two years later, Scott still maintained that those two people were a drag on the company and should have been dismissed. He did, however, regret what happened.

The two employees he wanted to fire had long been doing subpar work as was clear from their progress reports, logs, and revenues. His first act as manager was not to connect to the team to get an emotional reading nor was it to hear the team's ideas about good changes he could make. Additionally, he did not rally them around his positive vision for the future. His first act was to fire those two employees.

Scott said he called them into his office during his first hour in the building and turned to what he had learned in business school about difficult conversations. He said three nice things about them and then delivered the blow. With self-deprecating humor he admitted to saying something similar to, "You have great phone manners, you type very fast, and you make a delicious cup of coffee. The only bit of constructive feedback I have for you is that you're not very good at your job. Today will be your last day at this company." Thus, within the first hour under his leadership, he had eliminated the two biggest hindrances to overall team performance. And while the entire team knew those colleagues were the weakest links, in the same moment Scott fired them, he also lost his team.

The fallout *for him* was tremendous. Word of the seemingly cavalier and blind firing with no warning spread throughout the division, and Scott was instantly branded as an uncaring, out-of-touch manager who valued numbers more than people. People who never met him felt as though they knew him based upon that one story they had heard about him. Many of his team members worried they too would be let go without being given a chance, and all the negativity led to a drop in productivity and engagement. Why work if they might not be there a week from now? A year later, Scott's team had the lowest Gallup Q12 engagement scores in his company, he lost two really good people to competitors, and his boss moved him to manage a smaller team.

Scott had no social capital to lean on, which is something you should have before delivering bad news. Had Scott waited a day or even just had a team-wide welcome meeting to say there would be changes but to expect an incredible next year, then he could have easily fired the dead weights. But he didn't build social capital first, and that was why he could not deliver negative news effectively.

Social capital refers to the resources that are available to us based upon the trust and willingness of our social networks to support our actions.[1] Social capital built during good times is invaluable during challenges. The reason is that when hard times strike, the people you have built social capital with do not have to first ask themselves if they trust you or if you're a good person. To them, it is a given. Therefore their brains can focus on what is most important—processing the challenge, brainstorming solutions, and taking positive action to move forward.

Social capital resources can include information, ideas, power, influence, trust, goodwill, and cooperation. A number of factors influence how valuable these resources become, including the breadth and depth of the networks, the need, and the timing. If you know people well in your networks, you can connect them to one another when a need arises, such as when there is a business challenge or shortage of an intellectual or physical resource. Colleagues see you as the person with resources, reach, and relationships.

Numerous studies have shown that having a robust social network can lead to more influence at an organization and financial rewards, including higher paying jobs and faster promotions. People who sit at the center of their networks as opposed to the outskirts also frequently make more money, so social capital can also lead to monetary capital.[2] Often managers who focus on building networks instead of simply churning through their daily tasks are more successful overall.[3] Social capital is an exceptionally valuable currency.

At the Institute for Applied Positive Research, we found that a strong predictor of people's happiness and performance is their level of support provision with others—which is one of the best vehicles for creating social capital. This caring approach to business and personal relationships can be one of the most effective ways to create social capital. Examples of support provision at the office include helping others when they fall behind in their work, initiating social activities, and acting as a listening ear. Engaging in acts such as these will lead people to see you as someone who can be counted on. We call the people who score in the top 25 percent of the support provision scale "work altruists," and we've found they are ten times more engaged at work than the bottom quartile (those who wait for people to come to them) and are 40 percent more likely to receive a promotion. (Test yourself on support provision using the Success Scale at BroadcastingHappiness.com if you haven't taken it yet. See chapter one for information and the exclusive code you'll need.)

Social capital mainly comes from positive interactions we have with other people. After we have a positive exchange or shared experience with someone, we record that person in our mind as someone likeable and favorable. Central to building a rich social network and high levels of social capital is to constantly engage in positive network-building activities at work and beyond. We build social capital by calling friends to check up on them, sending holiday cards to extended family, and greeting store clerks with a friendly smile. The longer or deeper the positive track record we have with someone, the stronger the ties our brain builds between the image of this person and attributes such as "trustworthy," "kind," and "helpful." Positive experiences with others add to our storehouse of social capital and, as a result, people will put their trust in us. Officer Simmons was able to build even a small amount of social capital very quickly simply by not shining a flashlight in people's faces and treating them with respect instead of as unruly children.

Social capital is your greatest asset. So how do you get it and keep it? First, you can draw on the stockpile of positivity and optimism you have been cultivating since practicing the strategies from previous chapters. But here are a few more quick and proven ways to augment your social capital and seamlessly incorporate social capital–building moments into your day.

SHARED ACTIVITY

Shared activity is the best and easiest way to develop social capital. The social ritual of sharing food, coffee, tea, or cocktails has been used to create social bonds for centuries. In medieval times, you were supposed to protect guests in your home who had shared your food or drink. During modern times, one of the very first activities people suggest to get better acquainted is to go have a drink together. The idea is: "If we share a drink, get to know one another, and bond, perhaps they'll have my back when I need it."

Think about it—don't you feel closer to coworkers that you've seen outside of work? You are less likely to criticize an author's writing if you've been to Starbucks together. (Want to grab a coffee with me?) It's not about the food and drinks; it's that a communal activity strengthens social bonds. Make an effort to regularly place deposits into your social bank account by sharing food or drink with other people. Shared social activities include volunteering, playing sports, going to a movie, or going on a trip together. The longer, more frequent, and more emotional the activity, the greater the deposit into your social bank account. With your children, quality *and* quantity of time are important. The return on your social capital investment is the highest you'll get for any investment in your life.

CELEBRATE PUBLICLY OFTEN

Be the person at the office known for noticing positive contributions. Too often we are so focused on the next win that we forget to celebrate the previous ones. If you read and practiced the strategies from chapter three, you are already an old pro at this. If not, try scanning your office for previous wins, such as satisfied clients, completed projects, and achieved sales goals. Try to connect a win from the past to a current project or goal. For instance, one of our clients from Kalamazoo, Michigan, recently told his team during a weekly staff meeting, "I know we are working hard to get the 2.0 version of the defibrillator ready for release. I'd like to take just a moment to stop and see how far we have come. Two years ago today we were launching the beta version to five of our clients. Not only have we been consistently receiving positive feedback since then, we have sold it to more than fifty clients to date. The defibrillator is being used to save lives in more than three hundred medical locations across the country. I hope keeping this top of mind fuels you as you work hard in these final weeks. I know it will for me."

Being the source of praise, inspiration, and motivation builds your social capital because people see that you record and remember the wins. They feel more connected to you as a result.

TAKE FIVE

Every day actively aim to have a five-minute conversation with someone in your network whom you don't know very well. Connect with a new person each day. You might have to get proficient at cornering people and starting up impromptu conversations, but once you get over that part of it, these conversations can become very fun. Try to learn one new thing about the person during the exchange. It can be business related: "What's the best part about the work you are doing right now?" or "How's that project coming? Is there anything anyone, including me, can do to support your success at completing it?" Or you can learn something more personal: "Wasn't the Cowboys game amazing this weekend?" The key is to have a positive exchange, because it'll make that person feel more comfortable with you and consequently build bonds.

CALL SOMEONE OUT

Recognizing other people's strengths is a strong way to let them know they are seen and appreciated. Strengths can include creativity, curiosity, humility, kindness, humor, leadership, love of learning, social intelligence, teamwork, and zest. (For a full list and a fascinating assessment on how to understand your personal strengths, check out the VIA Institute at ViaCharacter.org.)

Character strengths are parts of us that no one can take away and so, unlike praising people for their successes—which are here today and old news tomorrow—praising them on the fundamentals of who they are can have a much greater impact on them. Look for and praise people in your social networks for moments when they were courageous (your sales assistant got up in front of a group of clients to deliver a report on the latest advancements of the company's suite of products) or kind (the new intern stayed late to help a colleague in another department) or full of zest (the annual conference committee chair went above and beyond this year). Find a person's strengths and specific examples to cite and build the social capital that exists between the two of you.

You should spend at least fifteen minutes a day on high-quality activities that build your social capital. Otherwise, when hard times strike or when you have to tell someone something unpleasant, you might not have the reserves necessary to lead people through challenges or deliver negative news effectively. You can spend three minutes here and five minutes there throughout the course of the day to get to your daily total. Other ideas for building social capital we have received through the Share Your Story section of BroadcastingHappines.com include offering office hours, sending positive emails, having informal break room conversations, organizing professional development and learning opportunities, and even buying beer for a group of colleagues.

If you're an entrepreneur, consider scheduling a fun, informal dinner with other entrepreneurs from your area. One of the best ideas I've heard is about a Friday beer cart on the stock trading floor in London. When the financial climate went south, the beer cart funding dried up, but this manager dipped into his own pocket to buy beer for his team. He said it was one of the best investments of his life, and he's a professional investor. His team worked harder for him to rebuild the business and, ultimately, they were successful faster than other sections in the company. When the company went through restructuring, he was the one everyone came to for an accurate picture of the organization's future. It was all thanks to the social capital he had developed. If there were layoffs, people were sad but trusted him to care for the team. This was the opposite of Scott's approach at the beginning of this section. The bottom line is that you cannot deliver bad news well if you have not first developed social capital.

STEP TWO: GIVE CONTEXT

You need capital *before* delivering bad news, but *during* the broadcast you need both context and compassion. I'll go through them in that order. Whether you're a manager, a maintenance person, or a mom, when it's time to deliver negative information to other people, it is all about how you frame it.

One day I showed up to computer giant Hewlett-Packard to deliver a keynote on the business value of broadcasting happiness in the midst of challenges. Before I had even stepped onstage, an announcement had been made that layoffs were imminent. (Talk about a tough power lead!) HP was expecting to cut more than fifty-five thousand positions. Addressing that crowd, I explained that they needed this research more than ever to help them wade through the barrage of bad news that would keep streaming in. After my talk, to my surprise, a senior technology manager told me how he was actually looking forward to the restructuring. My first thought was that this person was joking or crazy. But he was neither, and his reason for welcoming the restructuring was actually very rational after all. He thought restructuring might mean he'd get a different boss. I laughed, but as he told me the story, I realized he was outlining how bad leaders don't talk about context and good ones do.

Whenever there were business challenges, such as a project deadline that seemed impossible to make, his old boss would deliver the bad news to the team in a way that left them empowered and optimistic that they could fix it. The new boss, Roger, did not inspire anyone, and what was worse was that he stressed everyone out. For example, Roger would say, "We are five days behind schedule. I need this now, so you have to stay late."

His former, positive boss could deliver the same message, but he would include context in a way that changed the way others received the news. He would say something like, "I know that everyone has been working long hours on this project [*previous context*]. And the work has been high quality [*understanding of effort*], like Barry's slide deck he just emailed out [*knowledge of specifics*]. We are currently five days behind the schedule that was set by senior leadership [*the who and what of the bad news*]. You might think they didn't understand how much work this project would be [*emotional connection*], and yes, they underestimated it, but we need this project to be a success so we can hit our sales numbers [*rationale for the bad news*] and not have to let any more good people go [*emotional "why"*]. So, I need you to stay late tonight. I know it means not getting to spend time with your family tonight [*emotional awareness*]—the same is true for me [*commitment, which is actually the next section*]. But I'm confident we can complete this work and that will help many, many families in this company this year keep their incomes [*meaning behind the hard work*]."

Yes, it would take the old boss thirty seconds longer to deliver the bad news, but the effect was night-and-day different. Some managers have a Band-Aid mentality to delivering news: Rip it off fast and it won't hurt as much. But good managers, like good doctors, know that if you let someone know your reasons for doing it, they will trust you and keep coming back in the future.

In order to successfully give context, and thus deliver bad news better, be on the lookout for many of the keys I highlighted in the section above. Provide details that indicate understanding of a situation from the perspective of the recipient of the bad news. Provide a full rationale for how the negative news came about and why it is occurring. Clearly provide proof through specifics that you understand the ramifications of the negative news. And, finally, set up a context in which the current status quo context can be recast more positively. This last one requires better "framing" on our parts.

When stressful situations arise, it is very easy to fall into two different types of framing traps. Too often we frame stressful situations in "narrow" or "binary" ways, and both are detrimental. Both frames stunt progress and stifle positive forward action. Narrow framing occurs when we only include a small subset of facts and possible solutions, leaving out some that could actually help solve the problem. For instance, if sales numbers are down, you might consider replacing your weakest link or demanding everyone work longer hours, forgetting that other options could include sending everyone to a sales training tune-up or pairing the weakest salespeople with the strongest ones for an informal mentoring program.

Similarly, binary framing refers to situations where your brain decides there are only two possible outcomes—and it typically involves a win or lose scenario. For instance, it might seem that because Tom has not made contributions during board meetings during the past six months, he has rethought his commitment. If the only options in your mind are that he stays or goes, you might be missing part of the story. Perhaps something has happened that you are not aware of that is causing his behavior. By speaking to him with an open mind, you might learn that he gave feedback three times last year only to be shot down, so he decided to listen more at meetings to fully understand the needs of the company. Going in guns blazing with a binary mindset might not only damage the relationship but also burn possible bridges before you even get to them. Regardless of how the situation develops, some people not only stick to these frames but also disregard important new information because of them. Their mind stays frozen in place regardless of how events and conversations unfold. The more rigid our thinking in moments such as these, the less successful we are in the end. The successful broadcaster is one who is constantly updating the frame he or she is using for the challenge.

Whenever I describe the importance of giving context, I'm often asked whether it's better to deliver good news or bad first. There's actually a scientific and definitive answer. According to researchers Angela Legg and Kate Sweeny at the University of California, Riverside, the vast majority of recipients prefer to hear bad news first.[4] This makes sense to me! If I know bad news is coming, I'd rather get it over with right away. However, from the position of the person *delivering* the news, the researchers also found that if you want the recipient to engage in subsequent positive, goal-oriented behavior (ie, do something about the negative circumstances) you should actually deliver the good news first. The reason is that when people hear the good news at the beginning and know there is bad news to come, they start to worry about what the bad news will be, and that increased worry makes them pay more attention to what they can do to remedy the situation. If there is nothing that can be done about the situation, you can just deliver the negative news first. So pick the order of the news based upon the reaction you need. For example, if a doctor needs to deliver a severe prognosis to a patient who can do nothing about it, she should start with the bad news and use the good to get him to accept it. However, if her patient *can* do something to get better, she should start with the good news, then move to the bad, and finish off with positive action steps the patient can take.

Another good example comes from my friend Gil, a natural-born positive broadcaster, who knows that instead of telling his parents, "I can't come home to celebrate Thanksgiving with you this year," he can find other facts and tell the bigger story that can help soften the blow: "While I won't be able to be there for Thanksgiving this year because of my work schedule, I might be visiting you in January and March, thanks to a consulting project nearby, which would be so exciting."

The context Gil provides allows his parents to feel hope rather than merely frustration at not getting to see him sooner. Gil gives the bad news, which his parents can't do anything about, but leaves the conversation on a high note by noting his plans to return twice in the next year.

As you're framing the context in your mind, remember to do the following:

- Check that you're maintaining an open mind. Recognize if you are maintaining flexibility about a situation and leaving room for new information.
- Scan the environment for other options to consider. Actively seek out new information or potential solutions.
- Use more energizing words to describe the situation so that it activates instead of paralyzes you and others.

People often think of events, such as a performance review, as merely negative, but it is an opportunity to gain social capital and create positive forward progress. It is your chance to explain how you or the company arrived at the negative feedback. You can explain the process so that the employee sees the logic behind the conclusions drawn (assuming the process is fair). People are more willing to accept feedback when they find that the person delivering it is reliable and has good intentions and that the process used to develop the feedback is fair.

Often just the act of recognizing how you're framing something can cause you to evaluate whether it is working for you or not and whether you need to make adjustments. Developing awareness about what is often an automatic process can help you find the frames that work best for you, long before you need to deliver the bad news.

STEP THREE: EXPRESS COMPASSION

Like most people, I hate getting stuck on a delayed flight, especially when I'm impatient to get home. Since I travel quite frequently for work, I have some good war stories—delays, cancellations, reroutes, and even airport shutdowns with a four-month-old infant in tow (got to love O'Hare!). But even with those flying dramas, I have never experienced what JetBlue passengers endured one snowy day in February 2007.

You might remember this story because it made headlines for more than a week. Thousands of passengers got stranded aboard a number of JetBlue planes at John F. Kennedy International Airport in New York. A snowstorm had shut down the runway and many of the planes became iced over and frozen in place. The air inside was hot and stuffy, food and water supplies aboard dwindled, and the bathrooms became less than inviting. A newly-wed couple on their way to Aruba for their honeymoon said they remember looking out of the windows to see the terminal in the distance. They couldn't get to their beach vacation, and they couldn't get back home. It was a wonderful way to spend their first night as a married couple.

By the end of the snowstorm, JetBlue had cancelled more than two-hundred fifty flights at JFK, leaving thousands more people stranded at the airports. Rebooking was near impossible, and customers were furious. For an airline that had spent millions to build a strong reputation as the preferred low-cost carrier, this icy blunder threatened to freeze out future bookings and profits.

That is until Founder and CEO David Neeleman courageously faced the music. In one of the best apology letters in airline history, and after his company did everything wrong, he did everything right. He used the Four Cs outlined in this chapter, but especially effective was his show of *compassion* for the anguish customers had experienced.

Neeleman's message to passengers began as follows:

We are sorry and embarrassed. But most of all, we are deeply sorry. Last week was the worst operational week in JetBlue's seven-year history. Following the severe winter ice storm in the Northeast, we subjected our customers to unacceptable delays, flight cancellations, lost baggage, and other major inconveniences . . . With the busy President's Day weekend upon us, rebooking opportunities were scarce and hold times at 1-800-JETBLUE were unacceptably long or not even available, further hindering our recovery efforts. Words cannot express how truly sorry we are for the anxiety, frustration, and inconvenience that we caused.

Neeleman was not Mary Poppins, sugarcoating the message. He was short and to the point—and clearly named some of the emotions people had experienced. He was a human being acknowledging other human beings' feelings, and in doing so he became disarming. People can't be *as* upset or hate you *as much* if they feel you get where they are coming from. Of course, his compassion would not have been as believable if he hadn't followed up with commitment, which is the last C, so let me pause the story here until we get to that section.

The best and most important thing you can express to someone in the wake of bad news is compassion. Compassion is feeling concern for another person's stress, suffering, or misfortune. The word comes from a Latin word that means "to suffer with," and so feeling compassion for someone is not simply feeling sorry for that person. It is coupled with a desire to alleviate their suffering. Whether you are delivering bad news or responding to a negative situation, compassion is your best friend. It puts you on the level with the people you are talking to, as opposed to leaving you elevated by your position, a podium, or a negotiation table. Remember Officer Simmons? Many of the people who had received tickets from him said that he smiled and made them feel that he was an equal to them, not a disciplinarian casting judgments from on high.

And it turns out that research supports Simmons and Neeleman's approach.

Researchers from Simon Fraser University in Canada found that during times of downsizing, high-performance companies that showed consideration for its employees' morale and welfare were the ones where employees maintained high levels of productivity.[5] Without that compassion and care, productivity during layoff periods plummeted. Again, it is not so much about the news as about *how* you deliver it. So many people are afraid to deliver bad news because they fear only more negative results, when research shows the exact opposite is true.

My favorite line from the Officer Simmons story came from his boss, who said that a lot of officers think they have to be cold or indifferent to be effective and that there is no other option. They assume people will hate the messenger of negative news. But his boss said that Simmons is proof that is false (twenty-five thousand tickets and not one complaint) and that compassion is one of the keys to his amazing track record.

A compassionate approach not only makes moral sense, it also makes business sense. In a study conducted by Duke University and Ohio State University, researchers found that significantly fewer employees sued for wrongful termination—4 percent compared with 17 percent—if they perceived the termination process was handled compassionately.[6]

The value of a compassionate approach can be found in many domains of life. A fantastic study done by a physician at Lexington Veterans Affairs Medical Center in Kentucky found that a simple hospital-wide "I'm sorry" policy, which gave doctors permission to apologize to patients in the event of suspected malpractice, saved the hospital millions of dollars in payouts to claimants. For example, from 1990 to 1996, VA hospitals without the policy paid about 627 percent more per claim on average than the Lexington VA that had the "I'm sorry" policy.[7] Doctors who remained aloof, explained away their actions, or did not report the medical error to the patient literally paid the penalty. Compassion in medicine can save hospitals millions of dollars a year, which is why it is surprising that only 5 to 10 percent of hospitals are estimated to have an "I'm sorry" policy.

Think about the last time you were angry, stressed, or hurt because of something happening in your life, and the person you confided in expressed compassion for what you were going through. Didn't simply being heard and understood make you feel a little better? If you need to tell your friend that you can't go on the ski vacation you both had been planning for a year, expressing compassion for her disappointment can help shift her response from anger to understanding. As you talk to your child who is doing poorly in chemistry, try saying that you feel his frustration, or that you understand that chemistry is harder for some people than others, or that you know she would rather be playing with friends than balancing formulas—all of these sentiments create connections rather than hierarchical mental barriers. Delivering bad news starts with being human. Being human begins with expressing empathy for the suffering of others rather than remaining unaffected. Compassion is the gateway to great connection in the face of unfavorable circumstances.

STEP FOUR: STAY COMMITTED

Let us return momentarily to the JetBlue story. After expressing compassion to the frustrated fliers, JetBlue would have lost a ton of social capital had CEO Neeleman not followed up by staying committed to the recipients of the negative news. JetBlue pushed for legislation bolstering passenger rights. The company made new hires and corrected organizational processes to ensure that egregious delays would not occur again in the future. And Neeleman compensated the affected passengers even though he could have used the inclement weather as an excuse to deny refunds.

When you deliver bad news, you spend some of your social capital in order to keep the effect positive, just like how you spend money from your bank account. In order to make that capital back, commit to doing the right thing. When you express commitment to someone's well-being and to the continued success of a team or family, *and you follow through*, you may get a HUGE social-capital bonus check. Words are great, but actions build social capital ten times faster.

An important part of delivering bad news is showing that it is not the end of the story. A performance review that ends with the implied message "You are rated a two out of ten, you will be paid as a two, and I'll probably always see you as a two here at the company" will result in frustration by that team member and a belief that his or her behavior does not matter. A committed leader will provide the bad news in a different way: "You have been rated as a two, and you will be paid as a two this year, but I believe that you have the potential to be a nine or ten, and I want to work with you right now to outline how you can move from a two to a nine this year. I'll also call you quarterly to ensure that you're on track instead of just talking to you next year." See the difference? Make sure you leave people with not only the negative news but also an action plan. Decide what steps they can take to improve in a certain area and how the two of you are going to track progress. Be specific and remember that success is all about commitment. Your aim is to show that you are committed to his or her well-being and growth, and that you believe it is possible for this person to achieve it.

My friend Mary is a nurse in New Haven, Connecticut, who shows incredible commitment to her patients through extremely hard circumstances. Sometimes in the course of examining her young patients, she runs into cases of potential parental neglect or unwillingness to take the appropriate medical steps to ensure the health of a child. Mary occasionally finds herself in a position where she needs to call the Department of Children and Families (aka DCF or Child Protective Services) to report the parents or caregivers. Medical providers that call the DCF have the option of remaining anonymous to the family, which is an attempt to preserve the delicate relationship between the provider and the patient. Although many of her colleagues choose anonymity, Mary always gives her name for inclusion in the report. Not only that, she always tells the family the bad news herself: She has called the DCF, and the department will be investigating the family. She explains the reasons (*giving context*) and says she knows that it is frustrating, embarrassing, or inconvenient (*expressing compassion*). But the next part is key.

Mary stays committed to the family. She outlines exactly how she'll help, including to set up transportation if there is a court appearance, schedule follow-up medical appointments, call different specialists to ensure that care is being received, and provide ongoing counseling to the family. She tells them that if she sees positive changes she will go to court to testify for the family. Mary, like Officer Simmons, has never received a complaint. And in this case, instead of handing out a $100 speeding ticket, she is providing negative news about one of the most charged issues possible: an evaluation of their parenting. Yet even with such terrible news, Mary's commitment helps the family to know that this negative is not the end of the story.

Often opportunities to deliver bad news and show commitment do not result from circumstances as dire as a medical intervention. My father-in-law, Dr. Joe Achor, is a neuroscientist at Baylor University as well as a committed college advisor. Recently, Dr. Achor told me how he had a student who wanted to graduate this year because she wanted to walk at the ceremony with her friends and because she couldn't afford to continue taking classes. The only problem was that she had failed his exam and was failing another class in the department. She was going to be two classes short of the requisite number to graduate. Instead of letting the student figure this out a week before graduation or discover it from an automatic university email, Dr. Achor set up a face-to-face office hour with her and delivered the bad news: "You cannot graduate this semester."

The student cried and said she had no more money and her family was already planning on coming to her graduation. Dr. Achor expressed compassion for the student's situation, and then, importantly, remained committed to helping her. He called the administration and found a way for her to be able to walk with her friends, even though she would only officially get her diploma if she passed the two classes in the summer or fall session. And he got her in touch with the financial aid office, which could help her to take out a loan to pay for those two classes. She had failed, but the failure—if she corrected her behavior and worked hard—would not end in more failure.

If you've done an effective job at building social capital, it would be tempting to assume the people in your life already know you're committed to them. Don't assume they already know; reiterating your commitment to them can be a game-changer. While social capital tips the scale in your favor initially, communicating commitment *after* delivering bad news reaffirms to people that you're not only in this together but also on their side. It is also an opportunity to examine what has already been done and what else *needs* to be done to move forward. If you've already taken corrective action to help someone, this is your chance to talk about it. But you have to be willing to actually commit. A father who shows compassion to his daughter for missing her basketball game can use his stock of social capital, to promise his daughter that he will be there at the next two games. However, if he breaks his promise and misses those games, not only will he waste his social capital, he'll become bankrupt. Just as it takes seven years to overcome the credit hit after a financial bankruptcy, it may take the father weeks or even years to repair his social credit standing.

A humorous example of this is when CNN reported that a Falcons fan had, earlier in the 2015 season, said that if the Falcons somehow ended up with a 6–10 record, he would eat his hat. The team had potential, but in the end the Falcons collapsed and, wouldn't you know it, ended up 6–10. This fan ended up either having to eat his words or his hat. He chose to be committed to his word. On YouTube.com, he ate his entire hat and did not spit it out. So be careful what you commit to!

CONCLUSION

John Lennon is credited with saying, "Everything will be okay in the end. If it's not okay, it's not the end." When hard times strike, it doesn't automatically need to signal worse times ahead, especially if you deliver bad news better. Bad news is not the end of the story. Oftentimes it is just the beginning. Restructuring can actually be something that bonds people together. A poor performance review or a critical error might offer the chance for growth and deeper connection. Telling a friend he needs to hit the gym because his belly is getting too big could mean saving a life.

But here is the most important part of all of this. If you create social capital, provide context, show compassion, and remain committed, you end up reaping huge amounts of social capital in the future. When you show up for the basketball games after committing to being there, your family deposits even more trust into your social capital account. And if you're a master at delivering bad news like Officer Simmons, you might even get invited to dinner.

((• KEY TAKEAWAYS AND EXPERIMENT •))

THE HEADLINE

Delivering bad news is a part of life, and it's never easy, but how you deliver information makes a massive difference in how it's received. Delivering bad news using the four Cs not only allows you to talk about the negative without sounding or becoming negative yourself, it also leverages these conversations to create scientifically better business and personal outcomes.

THE BIG IDEAS

Hard Times Are an Opportunity

Bad news is not the end of the story. Oftentimes it is just the beginning. The way we frame situations is predictive of the outcome. Mastering this skill will not only make you more charismatic to others, it will let you find greater peace through the process. You will be both more liked and respected, and delivering bad news better will help you create deeper social capital with others.

The Four Cs

The four keys to deliver bad news better are to create social *capital*, give *context* to the situation, express *compassion*, and stay *committed*. Use them to create better results when delivering bad news.

Step One: Create Social Capital

Social capital is the resources (information, ideas, power, influence, trust, goodwill, and cooperation) available to us based upon trust and willingness of our social networks to support our actions.

If you have social capital, when you hit bad times, people don't have to ask themselves if they trust you or if you're a good person. This allows everyone to be able to focus on processing the challenge, brainstorming action steps, and moving forward.

Social capital mainly comes from the positive interactions we have with others. Some ways we can create it are helping those at work who are behind, being a good listener and someone people can talk to about problems, celebrating publicly the success of others, and initiating social or shared activities.

By creating social capital, you are making deposits into your social bank account. The return on your social capital investment is the highest you'll get for any investment in your life. You should spend at least fifteen minutes a day building your social capital.

Step Two: Give Context

During the broadcast of bad news, you need to provide context so people can understand why it is being said or done. People are more willing to accept feedback if the person delivering it is reliable and has good intentions, and the process of getting the feedback is fair.

Giving context to the situation means you give details that indicate an understanding of a situation from the perspective of the recipient, provide a full rationale for how the negative news came about and why, clearly provide proof through specifics that you understand the ramifications of the negative news, and then set up a context in which the current context can be changed to the positive.

Avoid framing stressful situations in narrow or binary ways. By framing a situation narrowly, we only include some facts and solutions, leaving out the ones that could have solved the problem. And when we frame a situation in a binary fashion, we only see two possible solutions, and this limited thinking can damage relationships and burn bridges.

Instead, check that you're maintaining an open mind and flexibility, scan the environment for other options, seek new information and solutions, and use more words that energize and activate rather than paralyze and depress when describing the situation.

Step Three: Express Compassion

The most important message you can stress to someone in the wake of a bad situation is compassion, which is feeling concern about that person's stress, suffering, or misfortune. It's not merely feeling sorry for them; it's having a desire to alleviate their suffering as well, putting you both on the same level.

Let the person know that they're being heard and understood. Being human begins with expressing empathy for the suffering of others rather than remaining unaffected.

Compassion is the gateway to great connection in the face of unfavorable circumstances.

Step Four: Stay Committed

When you deliver the bad news, you spend some of your social capital. In order to keep the overall effect positive and to earn that capital back, you must commit to doing the right thing.

When you express your commitment for the well-being of the person receiving bad news and to the continued success of a team or family, and you follow through, you earn a huge social-capital bonus check.

Help them see that bad news is not the end of the story. Give them an action plan that shows you're not only committed to their success and growth but also believe it's possible. Don't assume that people know you're committed to them. Show them through your actions that you're in this together.

THE EXPERIMENT

I sincerely hope you never have to experiment with this strategy in your life, but seeing as how bad news is a natural part of the human condition, at some point you may be the one who needs to deliver it. If that is the case, apply the four Cs to the experience. In particular, sit down with a pen and paper or a trusted friend and go through the four Cs one by one to map out what they will look like for a particular situation. Plan out how you will frame the challenge in a way that gives context and shows compassion. Decide on specific action steps you'll take to show your commitment. And, of course, make sure you're doing what you can to build social capital even in hard times. And if times are good right now, keep this strategy tucked away in your back pocket and simply devote attention toward building social capital. It will pay dividends if and when the tides turn.

SHARE YOUR STORY

I always love to hear the results of your experiments. Please visit BroadcastingHappiness.com to share your story and get special access to additional resources.

PART III

Create a Positive Ripple Effect

No matter how positive your messages may be, without people in your network to rebroadcast them, your reach is limited. Transformational positive broadcasters cultivate and leverage their network so that when they wish to share a positive idea or behavior, they have an engaged network to help spread the word. Only by activating people around us will we be able to tip our teams, companies, families, and communities away from stress and negativity toward adopting a culture of optimism and action. In this section you'll learn how to create contagious optimism in your network and boost your signal so your positive messages go viral—multiplying your power as a positive broadcaster.

GO VIRAL

Generate Contagious Optimism

They call her Sparkette. If you didn't know her and you got into an elevator at Nationwide Insurance in Columbus, Ohio, you might think the woman standing there was a bit crazy. Chances are you'd see Sparkette standing in her professional business suit, maybe heading to an important meeting with senior leadership to discuss learning and development strategies, and she'd be carrying a frog. The fact that the frog is an orange stuffed toy probably doesn't make this sound any less unusual. But if you ask her why she is holding a frog, you'll understand why this "crazy" woman is one of the most powerful forces of cultural change across several Fortune 100 companies.

Sparkette gained her nickname because she carries Spark around Nationwide headquarters. Spark is a frog in Shawn Achor's business parable, *The Orange Frog*, who discovers he is turning from green to orange as he does positive acts. Over the course of the parable, the more optimistic Spark is with the other frogs in the pond, the more his skin glows orange. When challenges strike the pond, it turns out being orange is both advantageous and contagious.

Sparkette loved learning about this parable, but instead of sending out an email to HR and senior leadership about how much she got out of the positive psychology training, she took one of the Spark stuffed frogs and carried it with her around the headquarters—especially in the elevators. When her friends or other employees at work would ask why she was carrying the frog, she would give her "elevator pitch" for why everyone at the company could benefit from the research in the training. Because the frog was unusual and Sparkette is a dynamic champion of positive research, senior leaders would return to their offices after their shared elevator ride and email her for more information about the training. As a result, the training has been prevalent not only at Nationwide Insurance but other companies too, as word spread and more and more people wanted to hear what Sparkette had to say. Nationwide is one of several Fortune 100 companies, including US Foods, T-Mobile, and Genentech, that went through the Orange Frog training and proved that positive ideas are contagious and adaptive. Sparkette is part of the reason that the Orange Frog went viral.

Once you have a positive story or idea, how can you get others to help you spread it? Broadcasting a story has incredible value, but getting others to share it multiplies the effect exponentially.

We've all had experience with things that go viral. NPR featured a funny story on the radio about how "Gangnam Style," a ridiculous but catchy music video with a recognizable dance move, broke the view counter on YouTube. According to Google, it didn't actually break the counter when it went over 2.56 billion views, but the counter had to be changed from 16 bit to 64 bit to allow the number to continue to rise. When the founders of YouTube built the company, they never dreamed a video could get even close to that number on their fledgling website, but now with more than one billion users, it is no surprise there is potential for a video to have gained so much traction.

My husband's incredibly funny and poignant TED Talk is one of the most watched TED videos, with more than ten million views at the time of this writing, and he jokes that if it gets a couple more million, he's almost in "cute yawning kitten" territory on YouTube. In a world with so much competing for our attention (I just spent five minutes online watching cute yawning kitten videos for "writing purposes"), how can we get our stories to stand out, to be heard, and, more importantly, to continue to be shared?

This question is incredibly important because culture itself is defined by the stories we continually tell ourselves. For example, America's character is shaped by the stories we tell of "going West," "a nation of immigrants," and especially the "Founding Fathers." People debate the Founders' intents so much because the story we tell about them informs our social mores and judicial decisions. The same is true at the local or personal level. A family is a collection of experiences recorded in narrative memory: a family vacation, a big move, a divorce, or a tradition. Similarly, a person can be defined by a series of athletic achievements or a career trajectory. When we meet someone we want to know better, we want to know his or her story.

A bond is created when we open up about our greatest struggles, but to stop sharing there is to cheat ourselves and others out of the even deeper connection that can be formed—one that is built on the fueling part of our reality. It is imperative we also share the stories of how we *triumphed* over those challenges and experienced personal growth as a result. Equally important are the stories that showcase the things in life we are grateful for, the meaning embedded in our work and relationships, and the hopes and dreams we hold close to our heart. These positive, activating stories are what truly create and strengthen bonds between people and shift a culture to positive, causing levels of well-being to skyrocket. Positive culture promotes positive behavior, which in turn fuels happiness and success. But all this can occur only if the stories we tell have legs and create contagious optimism.

In this chapter, I'll tell you the six key ways to choose and craft a story to make it, and an associated behavior, go viral. Using the latest science from positive and social psychology, you'll understand exactly how to promote a story so others feel compelled to adopt it as the top story of *their* broadcast. I'll tell you how to target the group of people most primed to help spread your message and how to activate a potentially more important group I call "the Hidden 31." And, finally, we'll discuss exactly how to transform something from being a one-day mention to a culture-changing story for your family or your company.

By combing through research studies done at some of the top academic institutions and observing them play out at our clients' companies, we have been able to cull the six most important elements of a story to make it go viral both online and off. I'll show you how to use this information to boost the positive effects of your broadcast at work and at home. You'll also learn how to go from being one broadcasting tower to a real network, unlocking your full potential as a positive broadcaster by turning up the signal for your messages, empowering others to share them to promote positive behaviors, and shifting the culture toward happiness.

ELEMENT #1: ACTIVATE YOUR "31"

Finding a Sparkette is great, but for your stories to truly go viral, there is a special set of broadcasters you really need to activate. These broadcasters are crucial, because when they speak in favor of something—which they don't do often—everyone really listens. I call them the Hidden 31, and they are one of the biggest keys to broadcasting happiness.

In a cross-industry research study with *Training* magazine, we tested for optimism at work and, more importantly, people's expression of that positive mindset to colleagues. We asked more than six-hundred sixty professionals from a range of industries, "How expressive of your optimism or pessimism are you at work?" Thirty-one percent of respondents said they were positive but not expressive of it at work. I call these people "hidden broadcasters." These people are one step short of being positive broadcasters; they are already positive, but you need to turn on their broadcasting tower. If they choose to spread your message, the impact multiplies. The fact that they rarely speak up often means other people will listen when they choose to start broadcasting.

In the consumer world, getting these people to speak up can turn them into "enthusiasts," and that can have incredible business advantages. As a brand you would do anything to have even a small army of enthusiasts—people who have tried your product or service, love you, and tell their friends about you. If they write positive reviews for you online, they are worth their weight in gold. And since 79 percent of consumers trust online reviews as much as a personal recommendation when making a purchase, recommendations from enthusiasts help drive business.[1] In your life, enthusiasts help drive the spread of empowering news, fueling stories, and positive behaviors. Your hidden broadcasters could be hidden enthusiasts—and the key to shifting your company or family culture from negative or neutral to positive.

The most important step in building an army of positive broadcasters is finding out who is in your personal "31" and activating them. You can do it a number of ways, from formal surveys to informal conversations. Talk to the people you know and figure out where they stand on a topic and how expressive they are of their approval or disapproval. Too often managers I've worked with have fallen into the trap of focusing on converting the most pessimistic person in the room to positive, while forgetting about their "31." Instead of going guns blazing after the biggest detractors and the most Negative Norms, try inciting the hidden broadcasters in your life to become outwardly aligned with the positive. This will tip the balance of power in a culture from negative or neutral to positive.

Negative people need not always win the battle for culture. When I give talks at companies, I'm often asked, "Which is more powerful, a positive person or a negative one?" Is the dark side stronger than the light? We can scientifically answer this, but it's not the answer you were expecting. A study done at the University of California, Riverside, shows that when it comes to emotional contagion, it's not the most negative person in the room that brings everybody down—instead it's the person who expresses his or her emotions to other people the most.[2] The unfortunate reality is that often the people who are the most expressive are also more anxious or frustrated. This is why it is exceptionally important to activate the positive people in the room and get them to express their optimistic mindset and positive emotions to "infect" those around them.

In 2008, a chief technology officer found his "31," and it led to the electing of the next US President. Harper Reed is irreverent. He has bright red hair, a big beard, and black-rimmed glasses. His Twitter description leads with, "I am pretty awesome." And he was a crazy choice as CTO for the campaign to help get then-Senator Barack Obama elected—a feat that was, of course, not a small order, turning a relatively unknown outsider to someone occupying the most powerful political position in the world.

Reed decided to use a technique called microtargeting, which tracks connections between a voter's interest and potential for being impacted by an issue or piece of legislation. Using this information, he invited current supporters to share personal information, mined other available big data, and found a way to send them targeted calls to action with specific people that voters might want to email. For instance, if you lived in a blue state and had a friend in a swing state, the campaign might email you with a request to contact your friend to make sure he or she was going to vote for candidate Obama. To make it easier, Reed and his team even wrote the email and highlighted the issues that your friend might care about, which you could then easily forward or utilize the microtargeted information.

Here's why this approach was so important: People who already really supported Obama were probably going to vote for him anyway. No value to having their information. But what this method allowed the campaign to do was to activate the individuals who could be persuaded to begin actively supporting him. In other words, these people went from being inactive or unexpressive to being potentially active. Reed succeeded in getting the most enthusiastic positive broadcasters to convert the "31" in their lives, and you know how the rest of the story turned out. It is a technique so brilliant that now both sides of the aisle use it.

There is one last important detail about the Hidden 31. If you are a positive broadcaster but feel like the people around you are not positive, the research shows you should take heart. Thirty-one percent of the people around you at work actually *are* positive; they are just not *currently* expressive of it. Activating even a handful of your "31" can tip the culture in your favor to help spread your positive message or behavior even further.

ELEMENT #2: RAISE THE BROADCASTER'S STATUS

The most viral stories raise the status of the broadcaster who shares them. Everyone secretly wants to be in the club (except, of course, for Woody Allen, who said, "I'd never join a club that would allow a person like me to become a member," echoing Groucho Marx's famous line from the film *Annie Hall*). It's a natural human disposition to want to be "in the know." As you learned earlier in this book, the more intelligent, knowledgeable, or socially connected someone is perceived to be, often the more valuable the person is within his or her network. Therefore, the information broadcasters share is not only a reflection on them—it also builds or destroys their social capital with others. If you give people in your network top-quality, useful information to share, you'll not only be highly regarded by the people in your tribe—you'll give them the material needed to enhance their status with their audience as well.

Provide your network with smart, unique stories that help raise their status as being people "in the know." It makes them experts—with high social capital—as they share information with their networks. And the best part is the cycle will continue as the people they share your message with, in turn, share the news with others, making *them* experts in their own right. Therefore, putting your high-value stories in the hands of other potential broadcasters not only makes you and them look good, it gets your story out. The key is to include information that makes your activated broadcasters look smart. Find a story no one has heard before and share it with people who curate and broadcast to move it forward.

While consulting on a project for the Zappos' Downtown Project Think Tank on Education, I worked alongside a school administrator who armed her teachers with smart data to share each week with students. She believes that when students start their day off learning something new and positive about the world, their minds are better primed to learn (remember the power lead!). Every Monday morning she gave her teachers a positive message to broadcast to students in writing—preferably with pictures. She always tried to make the teachers look like rock stars in front of their classes by finding cool stories for them to share. Examples included: fun facts about the brain, a story about kids in India cleaning up their community using graffiti art, and the ways teens had become amazing at a sport or skill. The stories were all positive and told in a fun way. But here is how the idea was really genius: The administrator, via the teachers, encouraged the students to then broadcast the story to a parent or caregiver that night. Parents were asked to sign a sheet with the story highlights to confirm the students had passed on the story.

The administrator's strategy was brilliant for many reasons. First, it primed the students for positivity first thing in the morning. Second, students had the opportunity to be broadcasters by sharing positive information and practicing their presentation skills. And third, it gave students a story that put them "in the know" and gave them a forum around the dinner table as everyone else quieted down to listen to it. What started as positive stories that caught the attention of one administrator ended up going viral around her school and the wider community.

Both online and off, there are three types of people who deal in the currency of content: creators, curators, and consumers. Whether it's on social media or around the watercooler, most individuals are predominantly one of the three. During this stage in my life as an author, I spend most of my time as a creator as I write this book and other articles and conduct research studies. For a shorter part of my day, I am a curator, as I collect what I perceive as valuable content to share on social media (join me on facebook.com/michellegielan now to see some of them!), and I am definitely a consumer as I peruse news sites in the morning and my Facebook feed at night.

Typically people spend the majority of their time as consumers. The way you turn consumers into curators (and therefore broadcasters to spread your message) is by creating content for them to share with their networks. And the content that will spread the farthest and fastest is smart content that's fresh and new.

Status also comes from our connections and the groups with which we choose to be connected. If you happened to miss the viral ALS Ice Bucket Challenge, you missed people dumping a bucket of ice water on their heads after calling out three other people to do the same—all to support the ALS Association's fund-raiser. The idea was brilliant because it instantly made people part of the "in" crowd as they participated in a wildly trending event. And the sharers also looked good (though cold and wet) because they were willing to take action for a good cause: raising money for medical research. So participants received a double status bump thanks to this viral broadcast.

And instead of one video being broadcast, there were tens of thousands. Each participant had to publicly challenge three more people to dump ice water on their heads too within twenty-four hours or donate $100 to the ALS Association. Many people did both. Cleveland Cavaliers basketball star LeBron James got in on the action early, nominating his two sons and even President Obama. With LeBron and other celebrities as part of the club, the ice bucket challenge smashed records—raising more than 115 million dollars.[3] Creating a broadcast that puts people who participate on the "inside" can spur the adoption of positive behaviors.

The best part is that if you raise someone's status by providing something smart or valuable to share, you boost that person's signal as an effective curator or, as Malcolm Gladwell calls them, mavens. People will usually keep coming back to hear what mavens say, which effectively deepens and strengthens your own network. Therefore, one of the best ways to get your messages to go viral is to make other people look good when sharing them.

ELEMENT #3: COMMUNICATE
HIGH EMOTION

At this point in the book, you already know the aim is to share positive stories, but we can see clearly that positive stories don't always go viral, and oftentimes it can seem as if only negative stories trend. Not surprising, because an all too common strategy for getting people's attention these days is to shock them into it. Tell them the most sensational fact you can find to put their brains on high alert so they'll pay attention to what you have to say and take action. As you learned in chapter two, we know from neuroscience and social psychology that this is the wrong approach. The same holds true for the types of stories we choose to tell. If you want a story and associated behaviors to go viral, make more than just positive choices about what to share.

While common wisdom might suggest that people have a propensity to share negative news more than positive news, the science is beginning to show evidence of the opposite. *A study reveals that the more positive the content, the more likely it is to go viral, and that the most shared stories are both positive and emotionally arousing ones.*[4] In this outstanding research study, Jonah Berger, professor of marketing at Wharton School of Business, and Katherine Milkman from the University of Pennsylvania used a computer program that scanned 7,000 articles from the *New York Times* over a three-month period to distill what characteristics led to certain articles being included in the "most-emailed" list on the newspaper's website. The researchers controlled the study for variables including article placement, author gender and popularity, and the length and complexity of pieces, and found that the articles that evoked emotion were shared more often than those that evoked none—but even more importantly, the arousing, activating positive pieces were more viral than anything else. They found that the ones that were most shared were stories that made you feel high levels of positivity, including emotions such as happiness, joy, elation, and awe. In psychology speak, we say that they caused high positive and "emotional arousal." Because the emotion centers in your brain have been activated to the point of neurological arousal, you are more inclined to take action, including rebroadcasting a story to your network. If you held arousal constant between positive and negative stories, positive stories win both in high and low arousal states.

What that means is that if we want our stories to go viral, we should choose ones that evoke high and positive emotion. In the appendix, we look in depth at the implications the viral nature of positivity has for the news business. It is literally a game-changer. The same holds true for our lives. For example, at a conference for a medical services company, the organizers showed emotionally moving videos that brought the entire room to tears at the selflessness of a few doctors. The videos told the story of three doctors who flew across the country to fill in during personnel shortages and the emergency surgeries they performed. In the videos, the patients' families tearfully thanked them for getting there in time. Back-office team members who coordinated the doctors' schedules and travel arrangements watched in tears as they saw the magnitude of the impact of the work they did during long nights while they were on call. During the town hall discussion afterward, one of the back office staff members got up and said, "The next time being on call starts to get to me, I'll think about the doctors I just saw and the good we are doing." People realized that the staff's work, while seemingly routine or unrelated to direct care, was supporting miraculous changes in people's lives. And because of that, they overwhelmingly began sharing the videos with their families and friends—so not only did this story spread beyond the operating room and medical offices, it began infecting others too.

There's another great example of a positive video going viral online in a way no one expected—especially not the motley crew that started it. Tech giant Adobe Systems was releasing a new version of one of its products, and the tech team decided to make a video about the massive challenges they faced, including almost missing their deadline. In dramatic Hollywood fashion, they told the story of a group of unlikely heroes who were able to pull it off in the eleventh hour. The idea was to share the video internally, but someone suggested sharing it on the company's Facebook page so all the employees at Adobe could easily check it out. It was definitely an emotional story of triumph, and even though it was way too long (it could have been done in five minutes instead of twelve) employees very quickly started sharing it beyond the company. Likes on the Facebook post jumped dramatically, and techies from Bangladesh to Taiwan applauded the team. The producers of the video would have never guessed this uplifting story would have spread that far with such a positive impact on the company's perception.

Broadcasting positive, emotional stories doesn't mean ignoring negative ones. You can still talk often about the negative as long as it is framed with a positive, activating tone. When researchers from UPenn changed the framing of a story from negative (a person is hurt) to positive (an injured person is working toward recovery), they found that the positively framed stories were much more popular.[5]

As discussed in chapter seven, the framing construct one uses influences how other people process the information. It also influences the likelihood that people will pass along the story or take action. For example, there was an Indiana elementary school principal who told a story about something negative—the tattered state of her students' shoes—but did so with a tone that signaled to the community it had the power to fix the situation. She explained how teachers had taped and stapled some of the students' shoes back together, and since many of the families in the school community couldn't afford new ones, she wanted to raise money to buy each student a new pair.

The story went viral around her small town, and within three days, the fundraiser had surpassed its goal. The key was that even though she talked about something negative (the lack of shoes), she framed it in a way that connected with people through emotion (everyone deserves a pair of shoes with no holes, especially children), and spurred positive action (to donate money to help buy shoes for these children). Right before the holidays, the school not only gave all the students new shoes but also socks and snow boots. The story's success means it will continue to be shared in the community—and if you think about it, I'm rebroadcasting it now, which is another example of the value of viral stories.

ELEMENT #4: MAKE IT PRACTICAL

I clicked a headline on Facebook once; any headline with the words *shocking, insane,* AND *revealing* in the title must be important to read. But alas, along with the 21,387,489 other people, I had been duped.

According to data published by *Business Insider*, the vast majority of the most-viewed stories on social media in 2014 were what some call "click bait."[6] Unlike the "most-emailed" pieces from the *New York Times* that were mentioned in the study above, which also benefited from quality reporting, the most-viewed stories on social media often come from less trusted sources. This would explain why some of the top spots of 2014 were taken by quizzes such as, "Which US president are you?"; the equally philosophical, "What kind of dog are you?"; and finally, "What state do you actually belong in?"

I can save you some time: If you are spending time online taking tests thinking you might be a dog or a US president, you're in a state of denial. (Full disclosure: I am a bichon frisé from Texas who channels a bit of Grover Cleveland.) *The takeaway here is that your story does not need to be practical to go viral, but if you want your story to go viral* and *be effective, you have to make it practical.*

In the news business, practical stories are called "news you can use," as opposed to stories about car wrecks or random acts of violence. These messages give us the info we need to make better decisions at work and at home. Stories are more likely to be shared if they are solutions-focused and create a change in your behavior. Think about it—you might not normally share a story about research on the effect of gluten on a person's mood. But if you just cut gluten for the past three days and you feel happier and have more energy, you are very much likely to share the news story that inspired you. *Action begets sharing.* If you share the best data or information but you don't tell me what to do with it, the story ends there.

The most helpful, practical stories are often not "broadcasted" but "narrowcasted." Sharers often decide naturally to whom information is most useful. By microtargeting key audiences within our networks, we actually spend our time and resources getting the right stories to the right people—those who can actually make practical use of the information. For instance, when I was pregnant and reading tons of articles about how to have a healthy pregnancy, I would "narrowcast" them to friends of mine who were with child as well (five of them were pregnant). It would have been awkward if I had posted articles about night cravings on Twitter. So as you craft a positive broadcast, think about how you should use microtargeting for the greatest positive effect—and how to get your audience to microtarget people in *their* networks.

At my niece's elementary school, her first-grade teacher uses Facebook to narrowcast highlights from the classroom directly to the parents of her students. She has created a closed group just for parents and posts pictures of student activities throughout the week. For instance, the teacher might snap a few shots of the kids doing an interactive science experiment to share with the parents. Not only does it communicate a higher educational value, it gives parents practical material to ask their kids about when they come home. And anyone who has ever parented a first grader likely knows it is much better to ask about a specific activity than to just ask, "How was your day?" You'll get a lot more from your child than the typical answer, "Fine." The teacher's narrowcast acts as a helpful reference point for parents to start conversations, and it triggers excited stories from the kids about their classroom activities.

As I aimed to do with this book, I encourage you to pay special attention to make anything informational you share also practical. Be explicit as you let people know what they can do with that information. Positive news is good. Positive news you can use is better. Positive news you can use that other people will help spread is best. Make others into experts by handing them smart, practical content in an easily sharable format.

ELEMENT #5: LOWER THE ACTIVATION ENERGY

My husband, Shawn, still sometimes sleeps in his gym clothes. In his book *The Happiness Advantage*, he confesses that in order to make it to the gym first thing in the morning, he would sleep in his gym clothes during grad school. The jokes about this have changed over the years. Before he knew me he would say, "My mom wonders why I'm still single." After we started dating, it morphed into, "No wonder I'm not married yet." Now he can't say anything! Anyway, the reason I tell you about his quirky habit is that he was applying one of the principles from his book called the 20-Second Rule: Make a positive habit between three and twenty seconds easier to start, and you lower the activation energy needed to kick off the new behavior. Make a negative habit a little bit harder to do, and you will probably engage in that behavior less often. For instance, hide the chips in the back of the closet, making them harder to get to, and you'll tip the environment in favor of healthier eating. Place a bowl of fruit on the kitchen counter, and the choice to eat well becomes even easier. When it comes to spreading your positive story around, making it easier for other people to share the information with their networks, both online and offline, helps increase how viral your story ultimately becomes.

The key is to package positive stories in a way that can be easily shared. Give people a headline that draws interest and put your stories in a format that makes them easy for people to discuss or forward on to other people. Lower the activation energy they need to expend to pass along the information. In our work, we love infographics—short graphical representations of information—because they turn anyone into an expert and are easily shared. We've seen companies create infographics as marketing tools to share online. Our partner Happify, which specializes in offering online games and activities based on research that helps you build the skills for lasting happiness, regularly puts out infographics related to the science of happiness.

What follows is an example based on concepts in this book. (For a digital version to share with friends and colleagues, visit BroadcastingHappiness.com.)

How Broadcasting Happiness Fuels Success

The messages we choose to broadcast both on- and offline not only predict our levels of happiness and success, but that of the people in our lives.

 Our words have the power to fuel performance and influence business and educational outcomes.

Studies show expressing a positive outlook improves:

| Engagement | Intelligence | Energy | Profitability |

Having a positive outlook can lead to getting an accurate result **19%** faster.

Beginning your meeting by praising a team member's recent success can raise team performance by **31%**.

Employees who focus on the positive receive **25%** higher performance ratings.

Optimistic salespeople outsell their negative coworkers, reporting **37%** higher sales.

Changing your mindset by viewing stress as **enhancing**, and as a tool to help you focus in the face of challenges, rather than as **debilitating** and as a roadblock to success, can lead to a **23%** reduction in stress-related symptoms, like headaches and fatigue.

1. The Power Lead

Begin a conversation in a positive, optimistic way:

Start a meeting with the company's recent wins.

When someone asks how you're doing, look for something positive and helpful to share rather than automatically replying "I'm fine."

2. Send a Positive Email

A brief email sent to a team member praising his or her recent success can really set the tone for continued high performance and create a positive work environment. By focusing on what's going right, you encourage future success.

3. Make a Gratitude Board

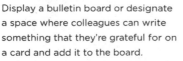

Display a bulletin board or designate a space where colleagues can write something that they're grateful for on a card and add it to the board.

It's a great way to make a strong visual impact that shows your team focuses on success, while getting employees in the habit of scanning for the positive.

You are a broadcaster, and with that comes great power and responsibility. The messages we choose to broadcast shape others' views of the world and how they operate within it. Broadcast Happiness to fuel success.

Brought to you by

happify™

Build skills for a happier life with fun, science-based activities and games at www.happify.com

Happify has operationalized the research that we do (see the next section for more about this approach)—and does it brilliantly. To put the science of broadcasting happiness into practice, I strongly encourage you to check out its platform at Happify.com.

In business, infographics and short ebooks provide smart data in small, bite-sized chunks, and they are perfect resources for people to share with their networks. With ebooks such as "10 SEO Myths that You Should Forget in 2015" and "How to Rock a Meeting," people can learn some great habits and easily put these practical pieces of information into practice. Tailor resources like this to your company, team, or family, and you'll be able to deliver stories, successes, and best practices that will not only engage your audience but motivate them to share the resources too.

Telling a pregnant woman that taking vitamins is good for the fetus is useful. Tell her—a woman who is too exhausted to research online for hours—exactly which brands come highly recommended and the doses to take, and you've lowered the level of activation required for her to make a change. Remember—and this should become a mantra for positive broadcasters—action begets sharing. If you get a change in behavior, sharing follows. Know your audience. Lay out the steps they need to incorporate the information into their lives. Decrease the activation energy required. The more practical the information, the greater the likelihood they will pass it along.

At a marketing company in Florida, Rose has become a master at creating information that her teams can "narrowcast" to their team or clients and serves it to them in a ready-to-use format. As the Southern regional marketing team manager, she often asks her consultants to share with her the secrets to their successes or recent interesting stories from their accounts, and then she creates a one-page graphical report to blast out to reps all over the country. The reports contain smart data that the reps can use to be better at their jobs, which is to raise business outcomes, including sales. Her most recent piece, "5 Ways We Dazzle Clients," gave quick snapshots of the five best ways her reps had wowed customers during the past quarter. These unique, motivating ideas and positive behaviors not only made for an interesting read, but also went viral as other reps learned and tried out the strategies. Additionally, the data in many of these reports was ideal to share with clients (with a few tweaks the story becomes "5 Product Improvements that Make Life Better"), so sometimes the reps forwarded them to clients so they could see the increased value the company is providing to them.

ELEMENT #6: OPERATIONALIZE THE MESSAGE

Effective positive stories don't come along every day, so once you find one, use it for all it's worth. If you're just telling it once or twice, you'll never realize the full potential it has to help ignite and sustain positive behavior. Not only is repeating the message important but operationalizing it to get others involved can get you the most out of the story.

I saw this in action in Cabo San Lucas, Mexico, when I was invited to give a talk at a fancy beach resort (the best kind of speaking engagements). During beach getaways, people are normally encouraged to put away their phones and disconnect from technology to find happiness. At this conference, organizers Lynn Randall and Melissa Van Dyke from the Incentive Research Foundation took a different approach: They encouraged people to get up close and personal with their phones on an app especially created for the weekend experience. Randall and Van Dyke knew the broadcasting happiness research well; to make the experience in Mexico meaningful and memorable, they needed to get people to actively participate in behavioral changes, not just mindset tweaks. Attendees were encouraged to use the app to take part in a "happiness game." They would win points by engaging in a variety of activities, including posting a picture of their "happy place" at the resort, posting a note with three things they were grateful for, tweeting about a fun vacation activity, and sending a complimentary message to another attendee or sponsor.

There was a leaderboard—and the competition was fierce! Being a software and tech geek, I was blown away that there was an 86 percent adoption rate, with nearly four hundred people participating. On average, each user spent more than an hour using the app throughout the course of the weekend, which was remarkable given how packed the schedule was with fun things to do. But even more telling was that the people who had played the happiness game, in the end, reported a more positive overall experience and gave higher ratings to all forty-two measured aspects of the event compared with those who did not use the app. By getting people involved in happiness activities, the organizers dramatically shifted how everyone experienced the weekend.

Here's another example—declaring "We are grateful" on behalf of an organization is good. Operationalizing that message by making a "gratitude board" at the office for other people to post things on it they are grateful for is better. Operationalizing gratitude in many different ways, which creates an active cycle of positive behavior and reinforcement to get the most from the message, is best.

For instance, you can do the following:

- Ask people to post their gratitudes on the board.
- Have them snap pictures of themselves holding index cards with their gratitudes written on them. Encourage them to post the photos on social media.

- Have a different employee each day share his or her gratitude with the team during the morning meeting.
- Showcase some of the "praise" gratitudes during team meetings.
- Have a volunteer from the design team create an infographic, with the organization's logo, that focuses on the scientific value of practicing gratitude to share with the company.
- Tweet out one gratitude from the wall each day to the wider network.
- Make a video to share the story of the creation of the gratitude wall and its impact to present at an organization-wide gathering.
- Ask a few marketing associates to record reactions on camera from people after seeing their names and contributions mentioned on the gratitude board. Put together a short video to share.
- Feature the story of the gratitude board in the company newsletter.
- Start each month with a fresh board and a new theme, such as "my coworkers" or "the difference we make together."

A comprehensive approach like this takes the gratitude board from a fun activity to a culture-shifting idea. One of the best examples I know is the story of a judge from Nebraska, who said her colleagues were disconnected and grumpy. After hearing one of my talks, she secretly posted a gratitude board at the office and provided markers and Post-it notes. Later, she told me she watched as colleagues stood in front of the board, sipped their coffees, and talked about the gratitudes that had been posted. Social connection, the greatest predictor of happiness,[7] was alive at her office like never before. She secretly snapped some pictures of people bonding in front of the wall and posted them on the board the next day with a note that simply said, "The bonding I see all around me today is my gratitude." The story of the gratitude board spread to other government buildings, and three additional departments made them too.

At a conference where I spoke to more than ten thousand sales professionals, organizers made a really beautiful gratitude board and professionally printed cards with the Twitter hashtag #iamgrateful. The board was completely filled just two hours into the three-day event, and the organizers had to put up five more massive boards to make room for people's overwhelming response. The gratitudes ended up on social media via the hashtag, and the MC stood in front of the wall and shared some of the tweets in a broadcast that was livestreamed to people who couldn't be there. The gratitudes were also featured in future newsletters, and at the next conference six months later, the MC read some of the best ones to the audience to remind them about the experience.

People at all levels of organizations have put similar gratitude boards up at schools, conferences, churches, and even parties to get people engaged in positive behavior. Nearly without fail, it ends up being one of people's top stories when they tell others about their experiences. And it is a story that can be repeated over and over as it becomes part of the culture. Viral stories stick when we keep revisiting them.

CONCLUSION

The goal of making a story go viral is that you want positive stories to turn into positive behavior, which in turn creates a more positive culture of infectious optimism.

At a group of hospitals in the South, there was something very contagious spreading from person to person. Normally that kind of contagion would be enough to bring out the HazMat team, but for this particular case, not only did the hospital administration and staff leave themselves unprotected, they also took part in passing it along. The result was a sweeping positive culture change that raised business outcomes such as referrals, work satisfaction, and even the bottom line.

Ochsner Health System had developed a severe case of contagious optimism. Don't get me wrong; it didn't spring up overnight. There was conscious attention devoted to telling a new story, making it practical, and operationalizing it to create the culture shift, but when it started to take hold, no one could stop it or its positive effects.

Ochsner was struggling with the same story many hospitals do these days. Instead of being seen as a comfortable place of healing and health, the first things that come to people's minds when they think of hospitals are diseases and death. Ochsner wanted to change that narrative. It wanted to be known not only for restoring health but for doing it in a positive, five-star environment. That's how it came to be inspired by the Ritz-Carlton Hotel Company.

The hospital staff adopted one of the things that made the Ritz-Carlton line of hotels so special: the caring attention from staff. You feel it especially when entering the lobby or walking to your room. When you encounter someone who works at the Ritz, they stop whatever they are doing, look you in the eye, smile, and say hello. The experience makes you feel really taken care of, even when you're miles away from home.

Desiring a similar environment, Ochsner imported that simple idea of caring attention to its hospitals. Training eleven thousand workers, it spread the story of how Ochsner was a thriving, optimistic place to work and stay. They operationalized the message by getting everyone to do two things: Within ten feet of seeing someone in the hallway, make eye contact and smile. Within five feet, smile and say hello. They called it the "10/5 Way."

This small behavioral change shifted the story of the hospital and transformed a place of sickness into a place of health for both staff members and patients. The result was a culture of contagious optimism. Not only did work satisfaction improve, patient satisfaction did as well. And since patient satisfaction with the care received is one of the greatest predictors of profitability, the bottom line increased as well. In 2012, Ochsner Health System reported $1.84 billion in revenue.

The chapter concludes with this story of contagious optimism to point out an amazing thing about broadcasting culture change: Once you become a master at it, it becomes unconscious. None of the patients walking into those hospitals learned the rules of the 10/5 Way . . . consciously. Instead, they picked it up from every interaction unconsciously. Then, not only were they reciprocating and participating, they actually started initiating the smiles themselves. It is my hope that both the research in this book and the broadcasts you decide to share in your life will make the choice to become positive an easier and more unconscious one for society. Because that is when change not only takes shape but also takes hold.

((• KEY TAKEAWAYS AND EXPERIMENT •))

THE HEADLINE

Culture is defined by the stories we continually tell ourselves. Positive culture promotes positive behavior, which fuels happiness and success. Getting others to share and broadcast your story multiplies the effect exponentially and allows you to go from a single broadcasting tower to a network of satellites, unlocking your full potential as a positive broadcaster. Creating contagious optimism can shift a culture at work or at home from negative or neutral to positive.

THE BIG IDEAS

There are six important elements of a message and the broadcast network that dramatically raise the chances of a positive story or behavior going viral, both online and off. Applying them can help boost the positive effects of your broadcast at work and at home.

Element #1: Activate Your "Hidden 31"

Research shows that 31 percent of employees are positive but aren't expressive. These are "hidden broadcasters." Hidden broadcasters are one step short of being positive broadcasters, and you just need to turn on their broadcasting signals. Doing so can make them enthusiasts, or the people who actively voice positive stories about your company or product. Because hidden broadcasters rarely speak up, people listen when they do.

Ask questions to find out who your "31" are and activate them. Figure out where they stand on a topic by asking them questions.

Get others to spread your message, but remember it's not the most negative or most positive person who has the power; it's the person who spreads his or her message the most and is the most expressive (including through nonverbal communication, such as facial expression and tone of voice).

Element #2: Raise the Broadcaster's Status

The most viral stories raise the status of the broadcaster who shares them. Information that broadcasters share is a reflection of them and either builds or destroys social capital.

There are three types of people who deal in the currency of content: creators (make the content), curators (decide what content to share), and consumers (take in the content).

You can turn consumers into curators by creating content for them to share within their networks. This should be smart content that's fresh and new and gives them the opportunity to be smart broadcasters.

By giving them smart and valuable resources to share, you boost their signal as effective curators, and people will come back to hear what they have to say. By making them curators, you've also just deepened and strengthened your own network.

Element #3: Communicate High Emotion

New research shows that the more positive the content, the more likely it is to go viral and that the most shared stories are both positive and emotionally arousing (that is, causing high levels of happiness, joy, elation, or awe).

To make our content go viral, we should choose stories that evoke high and positive emotions. You can still talk about the negative, as long as it's framed with a positive, activating tone.

Element #4: Make It Practical

Your story does not need to be practical to go viral, but if you want your story to go viral and *be effective, you have to make it practical.* Practical stories have news we can use, with information that helps us make better decisions. They are often solutions-focused. Stories are more likely to be shared if they create a change in our behavior, because actions beget sharing.

The most helpful practical stories are not "broadcasted" but "narrowcasted" to "microtargeted" key audiences. Give specific, useful information to a targeted audience and let them know how to use and share the information.

Element #5: Lower the Activation Energy

The easier you make it for people to share your story, the more likely it is to go viral. Give your story a headline that draws interest and put it in a format that helps the broadcaster talk about it and forward it on to other people (infographic, ebook, etc.).

Know your audience and lay out the steps for them to incorporate the information into their lives. Changes in behavior lead to sharing.

Element #6: Operationalize the Message

Repeat the message, get others involved, and turn it into an action in as many ways as possible.

For example, to operationalize an environment of gratitude at work, you could do the following:

- Create a gratitude board and put it on a wall at the office.
- Have employees snap pictures of themselves holding index cards with their gratitudes written on them. Encourage them to post the photos on social media.
- Have a different employee share his or her gratitude with the team each day.
- Tweet out a company gratitude each day.
- Make a video sharing the story of the creation of the gratitude board and its impact to show at an organization-wide gathering.

It's a comprehensive approach that causes a culture shift by creating a cycle of positive behavior and reinforcement.

THE EXPERIMENT

Viral stories stick when we keep revisiting them. Positive stories that go viral lead to positive behavior, and in turn, create a more positive culture of infectious optimism. Experiment with a story or two that you would like to see go viral at your organization, or with your family, and include all applicable elements of viral stories from above in your action plans. Use those elements to create plans that will engage people in your community to be a part of the story by spreading it. Notice the story's reach and how it influences thinking and behavior—and hopefully creates or reinforces a culture of positivity and optimism.

SHARE YOUR STORY

I always love to hear the results of your experiments. Please visit BroadcastingHappiness.com to share your story and get special access to additional resources.

CONCLUSION

It was a moment in time. Late author and poet Dr. Maya Angelou visited the CBS studios on Fifth Avenue in New York the morning after this country elected its first black president. I watched from the control room as she reflected on the incredible turning point in our collective history.

The most poignant part of the interview on *The Early Show* came toward the end, when host Harry Smith asked her to share one of her most famous poems, "Still I Rise." She began to speak, and what resulted was a work of art:

> *You may write me down in history*
> *With your bitter, twisted lies,*
> *You may trod me in the very dirt*
> *But still, like dust, I'll rise.*
>
> *Out of the huts of history's shame*
> *I rise*
> *Up from a past that's rooted in pain*
> *I rise*
> *I'm a black ocean, leaping and wide,*
> *Welling and swelling I bear in the tide.*
>
> *Leaving behind nights of terror and fear*
> *I rise*
> *Into a daybreak that's wondrously clear*
> *I rise*
> *Bringing the gifts that my ancestors gave,*
> *I am the dream and the hope of the slave.*[1]

Dr. Angelou beautifully concluded by pausing, smiling knowingly, and saying, "And so . . . *we all rise.*"

As she so eloquently recited the verses above with her deep, melodic voice, our director, Mike Mancini, wove in full-screen emotional pictures of people celebrating the results of the election. Together they brought to life a poem that had been written years ago, not about a black man taking office but about the "dream and the hope of the slave." In that moment I saw that, ultimately, they were one and the same dream.

It was a gorgeous example of broadcasting the beauty of humanity. In that moment, it wasn't about politics or President Obama or the color of his skin. It was about choosing a reality in which we are full of love. That morning, CBS News was broadcasting happiness.

Positive change starts with someone speaking up and broadcasting a vision of a new reality. From Rosa Parks to Mahatma Gandhi to Bill and Melinda Gates to Oprah, positive role models paint a picture of a better existence. A reality that is closer to love. As a positive broadcaster, you can be that person.

Common wisdom suggests that great change comes when we focus on the negative to highlight all that needs to change. It is now clear that there is an even more effective way to ignite and sustain change. This book has provided one example after another that point to a new, emerging set of operating instructions. Finding and broadcasting examples of what is already working in our world, community, school, office, and home can have even more power to transform the world for the better. Broadcasting examples of how others have overcome challenges gives us potential paths forward when encountering our own. Fostering and maintaining an optimistic, activated national and interpersonal discussion fuels future positive action and helps turn dreams into reality. Sharing stories of people like Officer Simmons at the Los Angeles Police Department or Sparkette at Nationwide, of places like Sunnyside High School and Ochsner Health System, tells people that success is possible and even shows them how to accomplish it. The most influential broadcasters among us transmit this kind of activating signal.

We need to move away from our obsessive focus on the negative. As mentioned previously, I don't advocate ignoring the negative. However, getting caught in its web does a disservice to our thinking, happiness, and potential. It changes how the brain processes the world and whether we believe our behaviors matter. Whatever news we broadcast—international, national, local, or even personal news—to one another, in person or online, shifting the balance of news toward the positive and transmitting a solutions-focused, empowered reality pays dividends on many fronts. It is what can help rid the modern world of all the ills that currently enslave us. Our words matter.

Each person who makes a choice toward the positive can tip other people in that direction. We are highly influential over the way other people process the world. For instance, just by changing what you broadcast on Facebook, you can alter what other people put out into the world. A recent study done by researchers from Cornell University, in conjunction with Facebook, found that when researchers manipulated the news feed to be more positive, people posted more positive stories in their own feeds.[2] The same holds true for the negative. With a sample size of more than 689,000 people, this was the first massive study to show the effects of emotional contagion. What it clearly showed is that what you broadcast changes the broadcast choices made by others. Your ripple effect is positive or negative depending on your choices.

Most of your influence on others comes as a result of the natural human inclination to want to go along with the crowd. Just knowing that others are doing something makes it much more likely that we will take part in the same behavior. This phenomenon from social psychology, called social proof, is when we follow what others are doing because we assume those behaviors are the correct ones. We see the proof that this must be the right way to act because they are doing it.[3] If you have ever been convinced to buy a product online after reading positive reviews from other customers about it, you have been persuaded by social proof. Studies have shown that people consider these reviews twelve times more trustworthy than descriptions written by the manufacturer.[4]

We take our social-proof cues from celebrities, bloggers, and people we know and trust. The most creative example of social proof I have ever seen in action happened when I went to see a taping of *The Daily Show* with Jon Stewart. Producers had a staffer stand next to the audience and laugh with a booming voice at all the jokes. At first it was alarming, but very quickly it caused us to laugh even louder, giving the audience and, subsequently, viewers at home the social proof (as if they needed it!) to see that the show was hilarious. Sticking with others feels natural and costs us less, mentally, than breaking away from them. We usually do it for one or more of the following reasons: We want to make good decisions efficiently, be like others, or get their approval. If you broadcast happiness and people see the positive results, your story becomes social proof. By modeling the broadcasting-happiness principles and motivating those in your community to do the same, you provide the social proof to other people that focusing on the positive and maintaining a resilient mindset in the face of challenges is the "way things are done around here." And as you've seen throughout the book, maintaining an optimistic, empowered mindset is advantageous. It fuels positive health, educational, and business outcomes—not to mention our happiness.

But that message is only powerful if other people hear it.

HEARING THE CALL

It was the biggest landing strip I had ever seen. And above Fort Bliss, Texas, I was flying solo in something just a bit bigger than a tin can.

I was arriving for the annual Fort Bliss Amigo Airsho. All I had to do was land a teeny tiny plane on the massive airstrip. Shouldn't be that hard or nerve-racking, I thought. Oh, how wrong I was.

The control tower communicates with pilots using special commands and phrases, which I was still learning. Add a busted headset that only worked on low volume, and it is no surprise what happened next.

After flying a hold, which is a fancy way of saying I circled the airport, I thought I heard the air traffic control tower operator ask me to circle again. So I did. We went back and forth as she tried to tell me to land, and I kept asking, "Sorry, control tower, can you repeat?" I could *not* understand her commands, until finally after the fourth try, she dropped the "fly-speak" and screamed, *"Land now!"* I barely eked out a "Roger that," before dropping altitude fast so as not to miss the runway.

After my tin can rolled to a stop at the terminal, I saw why she hadn't messed around anymore. Not sixty seconds behind me landed a jumbo jet. It was a carrier that was so big it was used to fly NASA space shuttles back home from the landing facility on its back. I am serious.

Sometimes we don't want to mess around with the message. Just like the operator didn't mince words with me, when it comes to getting your broadcasting-happiness message across to others, I encourage you to be crystal clear too. If people don't hear or understand your message, you cannot reap the positive effects of it or shift the social script using it.

Be intentional about broadcasting happiness. Choose not to engage in negative, gossipy conversations. Focus less on the problem and more on what can be done to solve it. When others come to you to complain, fact-check the story with them or use your leading questions to shift the focus of the conversation. Set the tone of conversations to positive using a power lead. Teach your kids an optimistic explanatory style. Continually build social capital with others through connective experiences. And turn off the radio or TV when all that is being transmitted is garbage. Rethink your definition of what quality news coverage means for you and the best places to get it. Choose carefully the stories you receive and broadcast to others. The clearer you are about your intentions and how you will connect with others, the more you'll reap the Happiness Advantage.

There should be more than enough good stories for your broadcast. According to Harvard researcher Steven Pinker, the world is safer than it has ever been.[5] Even though it might not appear this way given news of terrorism, food shortages, and other issues facing our world, according to his research, we are living in the most peaceful times in history. The murder rate, number of war deaths, and the percentage of the population dying of infectious diseases are all lower now than ever before. And life expectancy, quality of life, and percentage of the population with access to education are all increasing.[6] This is not to say our work is done, of course, but it is important to see accurately where we are and how far we've come so we don't get stuck in a fear-based mindset and reap all the negative consequences of it. Instead, let's build upon current successes.

In the news business, the time to make a great shift toward positive, solutions-focused journalism is now. News organizations and individuals that don't will go the way of the dinosaurs, because the changing landscape of how people consume news, thanks to technology, means a new financial model can emerge.

This model favors the coverage of more activating, engaging, solutions-focused news stories using an approach I call "Transformative Journalism." As I discuss in greater detail in the appendix, Transformative Journalism tells inspiring stories that showcase positive action people have taken in the face of challenges, while leveraging emerging technologies to not only inform the public but also to engage with them through discussion and calls to action. This new brand of journalism fosters an optimistic national and international conversation based on the belief that change is possible, thereby empowering people to take action. This style does not ignore serious events and issues facing our world; it covers them in a way that fosters optimism and forward progress. Transformative stories give the public hope that they too can make this world a better place.

Some news outlets have already fully embraced Transformative Journalism including *Live Happy*, *Success*, and *Experience Life* magazines, all top-quality magazines and websites dedicated to broadcasting the science of happiness and success. They highlight stories of positivity to prime their readers with the belief that their behavior matters, while providing tools to practice happiness instead of waiting for it to appear. It is a very different approach to the "if it bleeds, it leads" style of media. Many other news organizations are engaging in Transformative Journalism to a small degree, but there is still *much more* that can be done.

If you have ever been frustrated by the negativity in news broadcasts, I encourage you not only to read the Journalist Manifesto in the appendix but also to send it to the journalists and bloggers you follow. In the manifesto, I present a research-based case on why the public is ready for Transformative Journalism and why the business model and human psychology supports the shift. I also include the science-backed tools needed to become a Transformative Journalist.

New research from the fields of positive psychology, neuroscience, and advertising shows that abandoning the current disproportionate emphasis on negative news is not only better for society's forward progress, it makes much better business sense. The public is asking for something different and better, and this new approach will enable the news media to offer exactly that while rescuing the industry at the same time.

For you, the news consumer, the manifesto answers the two biggest questions: Doesn't negative news sell better than positive news does? And if not, why is everyone covering negative news? My dream is that the manifesto will be one of the very first resources aspiring journalists read in journalism school. In the meantime, I have taken my own advice, presented in chapter eight, about getting a story to go viral. On this topic, you are my "31," and so for you I have posted a digital version of the manifesto on our website (BroadcastingHappiness.com) and made it easy for you to share it with journalists, bloggers, and your network in seconds. You can be the positive broadcaster responsible for bringing about the change so many people have been hoping for. There are so many transformative news stories just waiting to be told. Be the spark that refocuses the media's attention on those life-giving parts of our collective reality.

And if they or you are struggling to see the other side of the news—all the positive stories that live around us—I suggest you simply head to your nearest airport and spend some time in the arrivals hall.

ARRIVING TO HAPPINESS

My favorite airport in the United States is in Norfolk, Virginia. There aren't many flights to many places offered from its tiny building, and you can't really get a good bite to eat once you've gone through security. But it is one of the few airports in America where many families still park their cars, come in, walk past baggage claim, head upstairs, and wait by the entrance to security for their arriving loved ones. You'll always find kids holding signs for their returning military moms and dads and couples embracing as sweet tears stream down their faces. It is the same beautiful humanity featured at the beginning of one of my favorite movies, *Love Actually*.

Hugh Grant's character, David, narrates as follows:

> Whenever I get gloomy with the state of the world, I think about the arrivals gate at Heathrow Airport. General opinion's starting to make out that we live in a world of hatred and greed, but I don't see that. It seems to me that love is everywhere. Often it's not particularly dignified or newsworthy, but it's always there—fathers and sons, mothers and daughters, husbands and wives, boyfriends, girlfriends, old friends. When the planes hit the Twin Towers, as far as I know none of the phone calls from the people on board were messages of hate or revenge—they were all messages of love. If you look for it, I've got a sneaky feeling you'll find that love, actually, is all around.

Love *is* all around us, and it is the most valuable resource you can leverage to ignite and sustain positive change. What we have been talking about throughout this book is how to constantly get reconnected to love. Love is the invisible fuel that activates us to connect with others and strive to make this world a better place. Love motivates people to have compassion for others and to do all we can to make their lives better. Happiness points to love.

This might all sound a bit squishy for a business book—but if we don't talk about it here, I didn't do my job. To ignore love is to turn away from one of the biggest elements of what makes us human.

The part of Hugh Grant's lines that stick out most to me is this notion that love-in-action is not often particularly newsworthy. While it might not be for national or local news, it should make the top story of our own broadcasts each and every day. We need to remember to share those ever-so-important stories of how love manifests itself in our own lives. From the manager's success-ful meeting with the team at the office, to the CEO's hard work that landed new clients for his small business, to the teacher who not only helped all of her students graduate but also got three of them Gates Millennium Scholarships, to the mom and dad celebrating their daughter's A in math this semester—let us not forget to tell those seemingly small, not-so-newsworthy stories to one another over and over again until they are cemented in our minds. Those successes become embedded within the fabric of our lives only if we broadcast and rebroadcast them.

There is love and beauty all around. What will make the dif-ference is whether we constantly make the choice to see them. And, more importantly, make the choice to broadcast happiness.

As stated in chapter one, we don't have to wait for the entirety of mainstream media to make the great shift. We can use the same strategies media professionals do to cover the news of our lives, and we can start right now with our families, organizations, companies, schools, and places of worship. We can do it in our news feeds on social media. And we can do it around the dinner table as we discuss everything from the challenges facing our society to the challenges our kids encounter on the playground. We do it by applying the principles you learned in this book.

Let's together make the choice to see happiness.

Let's together make the choice to broadcast it.

Just like CBS brought to life the concept of broadcasting hap-piness so poetically that morning in New York with Dr. Maya

Angelou, so too is my hope and dream that you bring to life this research. Without you this research is useless. Without you true change is not possible.

You are a broadcaster.

You are an agent of change.

You are the spark that gives other people the chance to rise ... and truly broadcast happiness.

THE JOURNALIST MANIFESTO

The research that I have been conducting with Arianna Huffington and Shawn Achor is ongoing and some of the findings were not available by the time of publication. The Journalist Manifesto is a living document, and it lives online. It can be found and shared at transformativejournalism.com. Here is a sampling.

THE HEADLINE

New research from the fields of advertising, positive psychology, and neuroscience shows that abandoning the current model of news coverage and adopting Transformative Journalism is **better for advertisers, better for the bottom line, better for the public's health, and better for society.**

TRANSFORMATIVE JOURNALISM

Some who have not thought deeply about the media mistakenly create a false binary: You can either have "true" negative news or saccharine positive news. But those are not the only two options. There exists a third path that will usher in a new era of how marketing dollars are spent and news is communicated to the public.

Transformative Journalism is an activating, engaging, solution-focused approach to covering news. It seeks to inform the public while providing the necessary tools to create forward progress. Transformative Journalism does not ignore serious issues facing our world; it covers them in depth in a way that activates the belief that our behavior matters, enables social engagement from readers and viewers, and provides actionable solutions to the issues covered.

Fluffy, saccharin, positive stories are not effective in creating positive transformation as they quickly lose viewers' attention and fail to motivate people to cocreate a more positive world. Transformative Journalism moves away from the current extreme focus on negative news to one that more accurately reflects the world, in particular by highlighting stories of successful action people or organizations have taken in the face of challenges that have led to success. Transformative Journalism fosters an optimistic international conversation based on the belief that change is possible, thereby empowering people to take action. By leveraging emerging technologies, journalists not only inform the public but also engage with them through discussions and calls to action.

The most common challenge to changing the status quo of news coverage is based upon flawed logic: If most news is focused on negative or sensational stories, it must be because this approach makes good business sense and because most people are attracted to this kind of news. However, **the duration of unhelpful models is not an indication of their validity.** Brutal dictatorships and slavery can exist for decades despite their cancerous effect upon society. And antiquated practices like leaving lead in gasoline or asbestos in buildings are changed once scientists do the research and people see the long-term effects of those practices. We finally are there with media, and in this document I reveal some of the research that shows that adopting

Transformative Journalism is better for advertisers, better for the bottom line, better for the public's health, and better for society.

But first, media is a business. It will not change unless there is a clear business case for why Transformative Journalism increases the value of advertising dollars and therefore revenue. The current state of media is based upon the belief that negative and/or sensational stories attract viewers, which in turn is attractive to advertisers intent on reaching the highest number of people. But as research has emerged, every part of that formula is scientifically broken. Real-world case studies show that Transformative Journalism raises ratings, sharing, and most importantly intent to purchase, and this is more attractive to advertisers who are now demanding quality over quantity, preferring sales to number of impressions.

Media is in its awkward adolescence, prone to teenage gloominess, caught in an obsession with the salacious, and hungry for fake popularity. But the third age of media will be marked by a grown-up, significantly more efficient business model in which stories will be shared in activating, engaging, and solution-focused ways. The work I am doing at the Institute for Applied Positive Research in partnership with Arianna Huffington and the *Huffington Post*'s What's Working team—as well as with journalism schools like USC and thought leaders from media outlets including CBS, FOX, and MSNBC—shows a compelling case for investing in this new brand of journalism. Not only will Transformative Journalism generate real value to advertisers, it will be better for society at large.

THE BUSINESS CASE

Groundbreaking research across the globe reveals that our current media and advertising model is inefficient. Advertisers wishing to reach the biggest audiences in the demographics with highest likelihood to purchase the product or service have been focusing resources on showcasing brands during news programs, in newspapers, and on news sites with the highest ratings/views. But the current formula for ad placement is failing to take into account one key element: the psychological state induced by the preceding or surrounding content.

While advertising researchers have long studied the influence ad placement can have on how people perceive the subsequently advertised product, it is only now that an incredibly convincing research case has emerged that shows that for media planning efficiency not only does context matter but, for the vast majority of products, context should be positive and engaging.[1]

In brief, research shows that a positive, engaged mental state directly impacts key measures of advertising effectiveness, including memory recall, feelings toward the brand, and likelihood to purchase. Studies show that engaging content people feel positive about results in more shares, attracts a bigger and better audience, and for the brand linked to this content, it leads to greater advertising effectiveness. Therefore, no longer should the coveted spot for an advertisement be the front page or the first commercial break simply because ratings are often the highest, because this is also often the place where content is most negative. A better use of resources would be to place the spot next to engaging content people feel positive about.

The following four major conclusions have emerged from the research and real-world examples from leading news outlets. Let's take a look at some of the research and case studies that together provide a compelling case for rethinking the formula for the business of news coverage.

CONCLUSION #1: Engaging content people feel positive about increases advertising effectiveness.

Positive, engaging content increases brand appreciation and likelihood to purchase. Studies show the context in which consumers are exposed to the advertisement matters greatly because it influences advertising effectiveness.[2]

In a study conducted at Stanford University and published in the *Journal of Advertising*, researchers found that print ad placement greatly influenced buying decisions. Consumers' attitude toward the brand was more positive and their intent to purchase was higher when the tone of the article next to it was positive, as opposed to when it was negative. Specifically, people exposed to positive content before the advertisement had a 24 percent higher intention of purchasing the advertised product.[3]

Fifty years of research shows the exact same pattern holds for television.[4] If someone feels good after watching a program, that person is more likely to believe the subsequently advertised product will make him or her feel good too. In a study conducted at McGill University, consumers who viewed a Heinz commercial during a positive show (as compared to those who viewed the same commercial during a sad show) were more likely to pay attention to the commercial while it was on and later remembered significantly more about the ad.[5]

Researchers from Cornell University and the University of Michigan found that when people process an ad in a positive mood as opposed to neutral, they experience higher brand attitudes, which are consumers' opinions of a brand. In other words, a positive mood favorably influences people's feelings about a brand.[6]

A study conducted at Ghent University in Belgium found that in general, consumers rated positive ads embedded within positive contexts as opposed to negative contexts as more likeable and more informative. On television, when the ads were placed within positively appreciated content, brand recall increased.[7]

Researchers from the University of Amsterdam in conjunction with Unilever found that programs that people watch closely and highly value carry over these characteristics to the attention for, and the attitude toward, the advertisement. Respondents were called after watching recent programming and asked to recall advertising. Viewers in the highest category of attention were 67 percent more likely to recall the advertisements than those in the lowest category.[8]

Herbert Krugman, longtime manager of corporate public opinion research at the General Electric Company, found that exposing viewers to ads was best done in the midst of engaging programming that they felt positive about. Ads placed in interrupting commercial blocks when viewers were very engaged and had good feelings toward the program perform better than the ones before or after the show.[9]

CONCLUSION #2: News can induce good or bad moods in minutes, thereby influencing how the brain processes the brand.

During a study I conducted with researchers Dr. Martin Seligman, Dr. Margret Kern, and Lizbeth Benson from the University of Pennsylvania, we found that it takes just minutes to dramatically shift someone's mood from neutral to negative or positive simply with news reports.[10]

Similarly, a study conducted at Kansas State University found that people exposed to broadcasts containing good news reported feeling greater positive feelings. Exposure to bad news left people in a more negative mood.[11] Meryl Gardner, Associate Professor of Marketing at New York University, says that the research reviewed by her indicates an "advantage to placing advertisements in contexts which induce positive moods."[12]

CONCLUSION #3: Positive, emotional content is more likely to be shared, thereby increasing the audience size and reach of associated advertisements.

A seminal study conducted at the Wharton School of Business found that while people do share negative stories, they are significantly more likely to share positive, emotional stories. Researchers Jonah Berger and Katherine Milkman from the Wharton School of Business at my alma mater, the University of Pennsylvania, looked at what makes content go viral.[13] They analyzed the most shared stories on the *New York Times* website over a three-month period and found that viral content follows three rules: Positive content is more viral than negative content, emotional content reaches more people, and people prefer sharing practical, useful content. Of the three dimensions, a news story's positivity was most predictive of sharing behavior. Highly positive, emotional content was most likely to be shared and go viral.

CONCLUSION #4: The public is choosing positive news content both in traditional mediums and to rebroadcast to their networks on social media, as evidenced by real-world examples from major news outlets and my own experience at CBS News and PBS.

As an executive producer of the national PBS program *The Happiness Advantage with Shawn Achor*, I watched as our lecture program on how to use the science of positive psychology became not only one of the most popular programs of the year, airing in 88 percent of US households with more than 2,500 telecasts, but also raised millions of dollars for PBS.

"Happy Week," the interview series I anchored and produced at CBS News in 2009 at the height of the recession, focusing on fostering happiness in the midst of financial stresses, was a huge success. We aimed to take an accurate picture of the psychological fallout of the economic downturn, while giving viewers the tools needed to overcome stress and anxiety. We got more messages from viewers as a result of that week of programming alone than we had from the entire year prior combined.

Longtime, well-respected journalist Ernie Anastos and his team at New York's FOX 5 WNYW began broadcasting a show centered on transformative news during the 6 P.M. timeslot and saw from inception to the time of this writing an increase in ratings, especially in key demos. The station has also received calls from other local FOX stations about replicating the model.

MSNBC host Krystal Ball's "Krystal's Kudos," videos that highlight individuals and businesses doing good for the world, get more likes and shares by far than any of the other content posted on her social media accounts.

Do you have an example of Transformative Journalism in action? Share it at transformativejournalism.com. And for the full list of case studies and examples, read the latest version of this living document online.

Taken together, the body of research and real-world examples makes a compelling case for advertisers to place ads with positive content and for news outlets to charge more for coveted ad spots that are connected with positive content, and *for producing the content in the first place.* For many news outlets, Transformative Journalism is the answer to shrinking audiences and dwindling profits, and will be what turns this industry around.

THE JOURNALIST'S WAY FORWARD

Change can start with anyone at any level of a news organization. You have the power to influence others by speaking to the world through your reporting. What you choose to say, the stories you choose to focus on, and the discussion you foster with the public can transform the trajectory of communities and the world at large. It starts by shaking off some of the long-held beliefs about what journalism is *supposed to be* and finding your new true north.

First, let's go back to the core purpose of journalism. "The purpose of journalism is . . . to provide citizens with the information they need to make the best possible decisions about their lives, their communities, their societies, and their governments," write Bill Kovach and Tom Rosenstiel in *The Elements of Journalism*.[14] The American Press Institute considers news a "part of communication that keeps us informed of the changing events, issues, and characters in the world outside. Though it may be interesting or even entertaining, the foremost value of news is as a utility to empower the informed."[15] News is supposed to inform people and help them make good decisions. Transformative Journalism builds on traditional journalism by activating the public and helping them see positive change is possible.

There are three tools you can start implementing right now to produce stories that are transformative: 1) choose optimistic, emotional stories, 2) tell the whole story, and 3) engage the public. I have included the latest research showing why, from a psychological or neurological perspective, applying these methods changes the way people think or behave. Just one word of warning: Studies show that reporting positive content raises the chances that your audience will view you more favorably. So, watch out for the positive effects this could have not only on your community but your career as well!

TOOL #1: Choose Significant, Optimistic Stories with Emotion

An optimistic story is one that might start with a tragedy or challenge but goes somewhere positive from there. When something bad (or good) happens, that does not automatically make it newsworthy. It is up to the journalist to explain why this story is significant and what people are doing about it or what can be done. Choose stories with an optimistic story arc that show behavior matters. Show indications of forward progress. If there is no progress in one place or with one group, show how that has been accomplished somewhere else or with another group. Optimism is the belief that negative events are temporary and local (affecting only one domain of life) and that our behavior matters. Optimistic thinkers expect good things to happen and take action to help bring that vision to fruition. Optimism is an activated approach to life, especially when it comes to tackling life's biggest challenges.

As an example, pension plans have earned a failing reputation, and in Illinois alone, reporters could do a new story each week about how these funds are mismanaged or falling short. Instead of simply featuring all the issues, the Better Government Association, a progressive organization, took a look at one program that was outperforming all others. "A Public Pension Plan that Works" is an in-depth piece on The Illinois Municipal Retirement Fund, which has $28 billion in assets and is 86 percent funded, much better than the next closest state fund at 47 percent. By explaining exactly how the fund is managed, lawmakers, fund managers, and pension program participants can learn how to transform their funds into a high performer so thousands of citizens can breathe a sigh of relief when it comes time to retire. This story offers context, significance, hope for success, and a potential path forward.

TOOL #2: Tell the Full Story

In the current news climate where a high story count matters, newspapers and newscasts are often short on space. While reporting, I remember fighting for an extra ten seconds for a lead story so we could include important information. Transformative stories include more information than what we have become accustomed to lately. Don't be a surface reporter. Find such compelling information that there is no way your producer or managing editor couldn't include it. For instance, don't stop at the tragedy; tell us why it is significant to the community, laws, or the justice system. Include smart data. Tell us the whole story arc. Revisit the story.

Haiti's earthquake back in 2010 offered the chance for the full range of potential coverage of a very serious situation. The earthquake measured 7.0 on the Richter scale, and when it was over more than 230,000 people had died. A number of news outlets covered the devastation by featuring heart-wrenching stories of the victims, one after another after another. What some of them missed, or took a long time to get around to talking about, were the stories of hope and action: the thousands of people who left their jobs here in the United States to volunteer, local fundraising drives in small communities that smashed expectations, and the Haitians who were able to return to some semblance of normalcy. The situation today is still very serious, and reporters can revisit the story. When they do, while showcasing all the work left to be done is important, even more so is including information on how much has been done to date. If all these years and billions of dollars later we feel that little progress has been made, there is no point in doing anything more because the evidence seems to be showing us it won't help. Simply reporting about the problems or focusing on how far we have left to go creates a psychological state of "learned helplessness," which acts as a demotivator and slows down forward progress.

TOOL #3: Engage the News Consumer

Technology has changed how journalists and news organizations interact with the public, and tech tools are the key to your positive ripple effect. Citizen journalists are becoming more common, even if people don't consider themselves one. People are reporters: The Pew Research Center for the People and the Press finds that 50 percent of social network users share or repost news stories. People are videographers: As many as 12 percent of people shared videos they shot themselves of news events. And people are pundits: 46 percent weigh in on news issues online.[16]

Engage the public in reporting and discussion in a way that fosters the spread of positive ideas and provides calls to action. Ask questions such as:

- "In your experience, what are the best ideas you've seen that can help remedy the business challenges featured in this article?"
- "Have you seen any schools that have effectively dealt with low attendance?"
- "What is one key idea you're taking away from this story?"
- "What do you do to get yourself back into a positive, empowered mindset when facing a setback? Please share your wisdom."

This is best done with users who are not anonymous. Asking these kinds of questions fosters a community of people interested in learning and growing. This approach gives people the opportunity to learn about new ideas from around the world and potentially put them into practice.

Technology also allows journalists to easily share resources with the public. Give people options of what they can do with this information: Donate to a cause, write someone a letter, share on social media to raise awareness, or import it into their work environment or home life. The possibilities are endless. While journalists need to be careful not to push for specific outcomes where controversy might exist, providing potential action steps communicates to the viewers that they are not spectators but participants. They have the ability to take part in making their world a better place to live.

A story done by NBC News' franchise "Making a Difference" on a young girl on a mission to feed the hungry is a perfect example of going beyond reporting to provide information to viewers so they had action steps to join the movement. The story centers on a ten-year-old who grew a cabbage in her backyard that ended up becoming forty pounds. She donated it to the local soup kitchen and fed nearly three hundred people in her community in South Carolina. Seeing those results, she worked with her classmates to create a garden at their school. The community supported her efforts by donating time and plants. And all the food grown there has been given to local soup kitchens. NBC News featured Katie's Krops, and families across the nation saw not only how a young person has the ability to do big things, but also exactly how to get involved by donating or starting your own garden. Young aspiring farmers could get detailed instructions on how to start their own garden. Five years later, Katie's Krops runs five gardens in her town, and other young gardeners have started seventy-five gardens in twenty-seven states. Viewers have donated more than $200,000 via Amazon.com's giving site. And in 2012, Katie was given the Clinton Global Citizen Award for working to end hunger.

"If a ten-year-old can think of an idea like this, imagine what other people much older than me can think of," she said in a follow-up story, and she is right, the possibilities are endless. The story of Katie's Krops is a fantastic example of Transformative Journalism in action and how to leverage technology to disseminate tools to people to ignite positive change.

CONCLUSION

A well-respected, forty-year TV news veteran recently posed a brilliant question to me: "As journalists, are we leaders or reflectors?"

To me, the answer is clearly both. We are both reflectors and leaders, but for too long we have been reflecting society's stories with faux leadership. Simply through story selection, fact selection, writing, tone of voice, and placement of the story, we have been making important leadership decisions that change what is reflected. We are leading people to see the world in a particular way. If we constantly focus on the negative, it is no surprise that what results is a public that is paralyzed and does not believe behavior matters when it comes to creating positive change.

In this twenty-four-hour, nonstop, churn-and-burn world of news, it can seem as if easy-to-cover, sensational stories are the best way to get your job done, please your boss, and garner ratings, but there is a new picture emerging. Technology is changing news consumption, and research is showing us the value of moving beyond simply covering negative stories or drippy sweet positive ones and instead forging a new, activating third path. What remains to be seen is which news organizations are going to be at the forefront of this transformative revolution in media.

Whether you're a journalist, producer, news executive, or news consumer, if you have questions about Transformative Journalism or want to join this movement, I would love to hear from you. I have set up resources and a contact form at transformativejournalism.com and invite you to connect.

The world is ready for Transformative Journalism, and you are the change agents. With the words you broadcast, may you find your true power as a transformative leader. Within you is the power to transform your reporting and with it, transform thinking and the world.

NOTES

CHAPTER 1

1   Margaret Kern, Michelle Nava Gielan, Lizbeth Benson, and Martin E. P. Seligman, "The Effects of Positive and Negative News Broadcasts on Cognitive Task Performance" (unpublished manuscript, December 12, 2012), Microsoft Word file.

2   Nancy Signorielli, "Television's Mean and Dangerous World: A Continuation of the Cultural Indicators Perspective," in *Cultivation Analysis: New Directions in Media Effects Research*, eds. Nancy Signorielli and Michael J. Morgan (Newbury Park: Sage Publications, 1990), 85–106.

3   "Increase Your Team's Productivity—It's FRE(E)," Margaret Greenberg and Senia Maymin, *Positive Psychology News Daily*, last modified October 4, 2008, http://positivepsychologynews.com/news/margaret-greenberg-and-senia-maymin/200810141081.

4   "Happy Employees Are Critical for an Organization's Success, Study Shows," Kansas State University, *ScienceDaily*, last modified February 4, 2009, www.sciencedaily.com/releases/2009/02/090203142512.htm.

5   Seligman, M. E. *Learned Optimism: How to Change Your Mind and Your Life*. New York: Vintage, 2011. Kindle edition.

6   Crum, A. J., Salovey, P., and Achor, S. "Rethinking Stress: The Role of Mindsets in Determining the Stress Response." *Journal of Personality and Social Psychology* 104, no. 4 (2013): 716.

7   Ellen J. Langer, *Counterclockwise: Mindful Health and the Power of Possibility* (New York: Ballantine Books, 2009).

8   Hochman, David, "Amy Cuddy Takes a Stand," *The New York Times*, last modified September 19, 2014, http://www.nytimes.com/2014/09/21/fashion/amy-cuddy-takes-a-stand-TED-talk.html?_r=2.

9   Cuddy, A. J. C., Wilmuth, C. A., and Carney, D. R. "The Benefit of Power Posing Before a High-Stakes Social Evaluation." Harvard Business School Working Paper, no. 13-027, September 2012.

10 Achor, *The Happiness Advantage: The Seven Principles of Positive Psychology That Fuel Success and Performance at Work* (New York: Crown Business, 2010).

11 Erbentraut, Joseph, "Don't Believe Everything You've Heard about Chicago's Most 'Dangerous' Neighborhood," *Huffington Post*, last modified May 23, 2014, http://www.huffingtonpost.com/2014/05/23/whats-good-in-englewood_n_5360688.html.

12 "Englewood Chicago," Google Web entry, accessed December 27, 2014, www.google.com.

13 Estrada, C. A., Isen, A. M., and Young, M. J. "Positive Affect Facilitates Integration of Information and Decreases Anchoring in Reasoning among Physicians." *Organizational Behavior and Human Decision Processes* 72, no. 1 (1997): 117–35.

14 Seligman, *Learned Optimism*.

15 Crum, A. J., Salovey, P., and Achor, S. "Rethinking Stress: The Role of Mindsets in Determining the Stress Response." *Journal of Personality and Social Psychology* 104, no. 4 (2013): 716.

CHAPTER 2

1   Bargh, J. A., Chen, M., and Burrows, L. "Automaticity of Social Behavior: Direct Effects of Trait Construct and Stereotype Activation on Action." *Journal of Personality and Social Psychology* 71, no. 2 (1996): 230–44.

2   Masters, J. C., Barden, R. C., and Ford, M. E. "Affective States, Expressive Behavior, and Learning in Children." *Journal of Personality and Social Psychology* 37, no. 3 (1979): 380–90.

3 Graham, E. E., Barbato, C. A., and Perse, E. M. "The Interpersonal Communication Motives Model." *Communication Quarterly* 41, no. 2 (1993): 172–86.

4 Howell, J. M., Neufeld, D. J., and Avolio, B. J. "Examining the Relationship of Leadership and Physical Distance with Business Unit Performance." *Leadership Quarterly* 16, no. 2 (2005): 273–85.

5 Lyons, J. B. and Schneider, T. R. "The Effects of Leadership Style on Stress Outcomes." *Leadership Quarterly* 20, no. 5 (2009): 737–48.

6 "Success Stories," Incentive Research Foundation's Incentive Invitational 2014, Quick Mobile.com, accessed March 22, 2014, http://www.quickmobile.com/wp-content/uploads/2014/11/IRF-CaseStudy.pdf. Additional details were provided by IRF in an as-yet-unpublished report.

7 Manfred Zimmermann, "Neurophysiology of Sensory Systems," in *Fundamentals of Sensory Physiology*, 3rd rev. ed., ed. Robert F. Schmidt (New York: Springer, 1986), 116.

8 Friedman, H. S. and Riggio, R. E. "Effect of Individual Differences in Nonverbal Expressiveness on Transmission of Emotion." *Journal of Nonverbal Behavior* 6, no. 2 (1981): 96–104.

9 Bargh, J. A. et al. "Automaticity of Social Behavior," 230–44.

10 Carr, P. B., and Walton, G. M. "Cues of working together fuel intrinsic motivation." *Journal of Experimental Social Psychology* 53 (2014): 169-184.

11 Bless, H., Bohner, G., Schwarz, N., and Strack, F. "Mood and Persuasion: A Cognitive Response Analysis." *Personality and Social Psychology Bulletin* 16, no. 2 (1990): 331–45.

12 Lerner, J. S. and Keltner, D. "Beyond Valence: Toward a Model of Emotion-Specific Influences on Judgment and Choice." *Cognition and Emotion* 14, no. 4 (2000): 473–93.

13 Dijksterhuis, A. and Knippenberg, A. "The Relation between Perception and Behavior, or How to Win a Game of Trivial Pursuit." *Journal of Personality and Social Psychology* 74, no. 4 (1998): 865–77.

14 Vollmann, M., Renner, B., and Weber, H. "Optimism and Social Support: The Providers' Perspective." *Journal of Positive Psychology* 2, no. 3 (2007): 205–15.

15 Staw, B. M., Sutton, R. I., and Pelled, L. H. "Employee Positive Emotion and Favorable Outcomes in the Workplace." *Organization Science* 5, no. 1 (1994): 51–71.

16 If you are familiar with my colleague and husband, Shawn Achor, you have probably heard the famous unicorn story. Yes, Dr. Bobo is Amy the Unicorn's husband—my brother-in-law. It's an unforgettable name for sure!

17 "The Healing Power of Laughter," HMDI Editors, *Dr. Stephen Sinatra's Heart MD Institute,* last modified December 30, 2010, http://www.heartmdinstitute.com/health-topics/stress-relief2/ 89-healing-power-laughter.

18 Bondy, E. and Ketts, S. "'Like Being at the Breakfast Table': The Power of Classroom Morning Meeting." *Childhood Education* 77, no. 3 (2012): 144–49. doi: 10.1080/00094056.2001.10522149.

19 Roxann Kriete, *The Morning Meeting Book* (Turners Falls, MA: Northeast Foundation for Children Inc., 1999).

CHAPTER 3

1 Loftus, E. F. and Palmer, J. C. "Reconstruction of Automobile Destruction: An Example of the Interaction between Language and Memory." *Journal of Verbal Learning and Verbal Behavior* 13, no. 5 (1974): 585–89.

2 Solomonow, S., and Gastel, S., "NYC DOT, NYPD Announce New Initiatives to Improve Safety for Pedestrians, Motorists, and Cyclists," *New York City DOT,* last modified October 21, 2010, http://www.nyc.gov/html/dot/html/pr2010/pr10_053.shtml.

3 Black, S. J. and Weiss, M. R. "The Relationship among Perceived Coaching Behaviors, Perceptions of Ability, and Motivation in Competitive Age-Group Swimmers." *Journal of Sport and Exercise Psychology* 14, no. 3 (1992): 309–25.

4   Grant, *Give and Take: A Revolutionary Approach to Success*, (Viking, 2013), 162–67.

5   Krugman, H. E. "Why Three Exposures May Be Enough." *Journal of Advertising Research* 12, no. 6 (1972): 11–14.

6   Berger, I. E. "The Influence of Advertising Frequency on Attitude-Behavior Consistency: A Memory-Based Analysis." *Journal of Social Behavior and Personality* 14, no. 4 (1999): 547–68.

7   III Roediger, H. L. and Karpicke, J. D. "Test-Enhanced Learning: Taking Memory Tests Improves Long-Term Retention." *Psychological Science* 17, no. 3 (2006): 249–55.

8   Graham, R. B. "Unannounced Quizzes Raise Test Scores Selectively for Mid-range Students." *Teaching of Psychology* 26, no. 4 (1999): 271–73.

9   Dempster, F. N. "Using Tests to Promote Learning: A Neglected Classroom Resource." *Journal of Research and Development in Education* 25, no. 4 (1992): 213–17.

CHAPTER 4

1   "Smoking Kid," created for the Thai Health Promotion Foundation by Ogilvy & Mather Advertising (Bangkok), YouTube.com, uploaded March 26, 2015; and "2012 PR Winners: Smoking Kid," Spikes Asia 2014, last accessed April 4, 2015, http://www.spikes.asia/winners/2012/pr/entry.cfm?entryid=2150.

2   David L. Cooperrider and Diana Whitney, *Appreciative Inquiry: A Positive Revolution in Change* (San Francisco: Berrett-Koehler Publishers Inc., 2005).

3   Diana Whitney et al., "Appreciative Inquiry and Culture Change at GTE: Launching a Positive Revolution," in *Appreciative Inquiry and Organizational Transformation: Reports from the Field*, eds. Ronald Fry et al. (Westport: Quorum Books, 2002), 130–42.

4   Ibid, 178.

5   Eichstaedt, J. C. et al. "Psychological Language on Twitter Predicts County-Level Heart Disease Mortality." *Psychological Science* 26, no. 2 (2015): 159–69. doi: 10.1177/0956797614557867.

6   Feudtner, C. et al. "Parental Hopeful Patterns of Thinking, Emotions, and Pediatric Palliative Care Decision Making." *Archives of Pediatrics and Adolescent Medicine* 164, no. 9 (2010): 831–39.

CHAPTER 5

1   *Age and Fertility: A Guide for Patients Revised*, Patient Information Series (Birmingham: American Society for Reproductive Medicine, 2012). The 2012 report still has the same findings as the 2003 report!

2   Dunson, D. B., Baird, D. D., and Colombo, B. "Increased Infertility with Age in Men and Women." *Obstetrics & Gynecology* 103, no. 1, (2004): 51–56.

3   "How Long Can You Wait to Have a Baby?" Jean Twenge, *The Atlantic*, last modified June 19, 2013, http://www.theatlantic.com/magazine/archive/2013/07/how-long-can-you-wait-to-have-a-baby/309374/2/.

4   Cooperrider, D. L. "Positive Image, Positive Action: The Affirmative Basis of Organizing," in *Appreciative Management and Leadership: The Power of Positive Thought and Action in Organizations*, rev. ed., eds. Suresh Srivastva and David L. Cooperrider (Euclid: Williams Custom Publishing, 1999), 91–125.

5   Youssef, C. M. and Luthans, F. "Positive Organizational Behavior in the Workplace: The Impact of Hope, Optimism, and Resilience." *Journal of Management* 33, no.5 (2007): 774–800.

6   Peterson, C. "The Future of Optimism." *American Psychologist* 55, no. 1 (2000): 44–55.

7   Aspinwall, L. G. and Taylor, S. E. "A Stitch in Time: Self-Regulation and Proactive Coping." *Psychological Bulletin* 121, no. 3 (1997): 417–36.

8   Peterson, C. and Barrett, L. C. "Explanatory Style and Academic Performance among University Freshmen." *Personality and Social Psychology* 53, no. 3 (1987): 603–7.

9   Seligman, M. E. and Schulman, P. "Explanatory Style as a Predictor of Productivity and Quitting among Life Insurance Sales Agents." *Journal of Personality and Social Psychology* 50, no. 4 (1986): 832–38.

10 Segerstrom, S. C. "Optimism and Resources: Effects on Each Other and on Health over 10 Years." *Journal of Research in Personality* 41, no. 4 (2007): 772–86.

11 Puri, M. and Robinson, D. T. "Optimism and Economic Choice." *Journal of Financial Economics* 86, no. 1 (2007): 71–99.

12 Seligman, *Learned Optimism*.

13 Srivastava, S. et al. "Optimism in Close Relationships: How Seeing Things in a Positive Light Makes Them So." *Journal of Personality and Social Psychology* 91, no. 1 (2006): 143.

14 Weingarten, H. R. "Marital Status and Well-Being: A National Study Comparing First-Married, Currently Divorced, and Remarried Adults." *Journal of Marriage and the Family* 47, no. 3 (1985): 653–62.

15 Christopher Peterson and Lisa M. Bossio, *Health and Optimism: New Research on the Relationship between Positive Thinking and Physical Well-Being*. (New York: The Free Press, 1991), 1–25.

16 Crum, A. J. et al. "Rethinking Stress," 716.

CHAPTER 6

1   Uchino, B. N. et al. "Social Relationships and Health: Is Feeling Positive, Negative, or Both (Ambivalent) about Your Social Ties Related to Telomeres?" *Health Psychology* 31, no. 6 (2012): 789; and Epel, E. S. et al. "Accelerated Telomere Shortening in Response to Life Stress." *Proceedings of the National Academy of Sciences* 101, no. 49 (2004): 17312–15.

2   Wild, B., Erb, M., and Bartels, M. "Are Emotions Contagious? Evoked Emotions while Viewing Emotionally Expressive Faces: Quality, Quantity, Time Course and Gender Differences." *Psychiatry Research* 102, no. 2 (2001): 109–24.

3   Barsade, S. G. "The Ripple Effect: Emotional Contagion and Its Influence on Group Behavior." *Administrative Science Quarterly* 47, no 4 (2002): 644–75.

4   Elaine Hatfield, John T. Cacioppo, and Richard L. Rapson, *Emotional Contagion*, Studies in Emotion and Social Interaction Series (New York: Cambridge University Press, 1993), 1–25.

5   Katz, J., Beach, S. R., and Joiner Jr., T. E. "Contagious Depression in Dating Couples." *Journal of Social and Clinical Psychology* 18, no. 1 (1999): 1–13.

6   "State of the Global Workplace Report 2013: Employee Engagement Insights for Business Leaders Worldwide," Gallop.com, http://www.gallup.com/services/178517/state-global-workplace.aspx.

7   Watkins, P. C., Uhder, J., and Pichinevskiy, S. "Grateful Recounting Enhances Subjective Well-Being: The Importance of Grateful Processing." *The Journal of Positive Psychology* 10, no. 2 (2015): 91–8.

8   Killen, A. and Macaskill, A. "Using a Gratitude Intervention to Enhance Well-Being in Older Adults." *Journal of Happiness Studies* (2014): 1–18.

CHAPTER 7

1   Wayne E. Baker, *Achieving Success through Social Capital: Tapping the Hidden Resources in Your Personal and Business Networks* (San Francisco: Jossey-Bass, 2000), 1–26.

2   Jeffery Pfeffer, *Managing with Power: Politics and Influence in Organizations* (Boston: Harvard Business School Press, 1992).

3   Linda A. Hill, *Becoming a Manager: Mastery of a New Identity* (Boston: Harvard Business School Press, 1992).

4   Legg, A. M. and Sweeney, K. "Do You Want the Good News or the Bad News First? The Nature and Consequences of News Order Preferences." *Personality and Social Psychology Bulletin* 40, no. 3 (2014): 279–88.

5   Iverson, R. D. and Zatzick, C. D. "The Effects of Downsizing on Labor Productivity: The Value of Showing Consideration for Employees' Morale and Welfare in High-Performance Work Systems." *Human Resource Management* 50, no. 1 (2011): 29–44.

6   Lind, E. A., Greenberg, J., Scott, K. S., and Welchans, T. D. "The Winding Road from Employee to Complainant: Situational and Psychological Determinants of Wrongful-Termination Claims." *Administrative Science Quarterly* 45, no. 3 (2000): 557–90.

7   O'Reilly, K., "'I'm Sorry': Why Is It So Hard for Doctors to Say?", *American Medical News*, last modified February 1, 2010, http://www.amednews.com/article/20100201/profession/302019937/4/.

CHAPTER 8

1   Anderson, M., "2013 Study: 79% of Consumers Trust Online Reviews As Much As Personal Recommendations," SearchEngineLand.com, last modified June 26, 2013, http://searchengineland.com/2013-study-79-of-consumers-trust-online-reviews-as-much-as-personal-recommendations-164565.

2   Friedman, H. S. and Riggio, R. E. "Effect of Individual Differences in Nonverbal Expressiveness on Transmission of Emotion." *Journal of Nonverbal Behavior* 6, no. 2 (1981): 96–104.

3   "ALS Ice Bucket Challenge—FAQ," The ALS Association, ALSA.org, accessed January 1, 2015, http://www.alsa.org/about-us/ice-bucket-challenge-faq.html.

4   Berger, J. Milkman, K. L. "What Makes Online Content Viral?" *Journal of Marketing Research* 49, no. 2 (2011): 192–205.

5   Ibid, 192–205.

6   Shontell, A., "The 30 Most Viral Stories of 2014 Will Make You Shake Your Fists and Scream, 'Why?!'", Business Insider,

last modified June 23, 2014, http://www.businessinsider.com/ 30-most-viral-stories-of-2014-2014-6.

7   Achor, *The Happiness Advantage*, 176. Kindle edition.

CONCLUSION

1   "Maya Angelou: 'I'm So Proud'," CBS segment from *The Early Show*, YouTube.com, uploaded November 5, 2008, https://www.youtube.com/watch?v=VIQPxBUDu8s.

2   Kramer, A. D. I., Guillory, J. E., and Hancock, J. T. "Experimental Evidence of Massive-Scale Emotional Contagion through Social Networks." *Proceedings of the National Academy of Sciences of the United States of America* 111, no. 24 (2014): 8788–90.

3   Robert B. Cialdini, *Influence: The Psychology of Persuasion* (New York: HarperCollins Publishers, 2007), 114–20.

4   Graham Charlton, "Ecommerce Consumer Reviews: Why You Need Them and How to Use Them," *Econsultancy* (blog), June 30, 2012, https://econsultancy.com/blog/9366-ecommerce-consumer-reviews-why-you-need-them-and-how-to-use-them#i.35yv7v2okfp7yq.

5   Steven Pinker, *The Better Angels of Our Nature: The Decline of Violence in History and Its Causes.* New York: Viking Adult, 2012. Kindle edition.

6   Zack Beauchamp, "5 Reasons Why 2013 Was the Best Year in Human History," *ThinkProgress*, modified December 12, 2013, http://thinkprogress.org/security/2013/12/11/3036671/2013-certainly-year-human-history/.

HOW BROADCASTING HAPPINESS
FUELS SUCCESS

1   Crum, A. J., Salovey, P., and Achor, S. "Rethinking Stress: The Role of Mindsets in Determining the Stress Response." *Journal of Personality and Social Psychology.* http://dx.doi.org/10.1037/a0031201.

2   Estrada, C. A., Isen, A. M., and Young, M. J. "Positive Affect Facilitates Integration of Information and Decreases Anchoring in Reasoning among Physicians." *Organizational Behavior and Human Decision Processes.*

3   Margaret Greenberg and Senia Maymin, "Increase Your Team's Productivity—It's FRE(E)," *Positive Psychology News Daily*, last modified October 4, 2008, http://positivepsychologynews.com/news/margaret-greenberg-and-senia-maymin/200810141081.

4   Seligman, M. E. *Learned Optimism: How to Change Your Mind and Your Life.* New York: Vintage, 2011.

THE JOURNALIST MANIFESTO

1   The research supports this approach for the vast majority of products and services. The exceptions fall under a class of products that one might purchase after feeling fear, such as home alarm systems, identity protection, or guns.

2   Singh, S. N. and Churchill, G. A. "Arousal and advertising effectiveness." *Journal of Advertising* 16, no. 1 (1987): 4–10.

3   Yi, Y. "Cognitive and affective priming effects of the context for print advertisements." *Journal of Advertising* 19, no. 2 (1990): 40–48.

4   Axelrod, J. N. "Induced moods and attitudes towards products." *Journal of Advertising Research* 3 (1963): 19–24.

5   Goldberg, M. E. and Gorn, G. J. "Happy and sad TV programs: How they affect reactions to commercials." *Journal of Consumer Research* 14, no. 3 (1987): 387–403.

6   Batra, R, and Stayman, D. M. "The role of mood in advertising effectiveness." *Journal of Consumer Research* 17, no. 2 (1990): 203–14.

7   De Pelsmacker P., Geuens, M., and Anckaert P. "Media Context and Advertising Effectiveness: The Role of Context Appreciation and Context/Ad Similarity." *Journal of Advertising* 31, no. 2 (2002): 49–61, doi: 10.1080/00913367.2002.10673666.

8   Moorman, M., Neijens, P. C., and Smit, E. G. "The effects of program responses on the processing of commercials placed at various positions in the program and the block." *Journal of Advertising Research* 45, no. 01 (2005): 49–59.

9   Krugman, H. E. "Television program interest and commercial interruption." *Journal of Advertising Research* 21, no. 1 (1983): 21–23.

10   Margaret Kern, Michelle Nava Gielan, Lizbeth Benson, and Martin E.P. Seligman, "The Effects of Positive and Negative News Broadcasts on Cognitive Task Performance" (unpublished manuscript, December 12, 2012), Microsoft Word file.

11   Veitch, R. and Griffitt, W. "Good News-Bad News: Affective and Interpersonal Effects1." *Journal of Applied Social Psychology* 6, no. 1 (1976): 69–75.

12   Gardner, M. P. "Mood states and consumer behavior: A critical review." *Journal of Consumer Research* 12, no. 3 (1985): 281–300.

13   Berger, J. and Milkman, K. L. "What makes online content viral?" *Journal of Marketing Research* 49, no. 2 (2011): 192–205.

14   Bill Kovach and Tom Rosenstiel, *The Elements of Journalism: What Newspeople Should Know and the Public Should Expect* (New York: Three Rivers Press, 2007).

15   "What is the purpose of journalism?" *American Press Institute.* (n.d). Retrieved from http://www.americanpressinstitute.org/journalism-essentials/what-is-journalism/purpose-journalism/.

16   Matsa, K. E. and Mitchell, A. "8 key takeaways about social media and news." *Pew Research Center Journalism & Media.* (2014). Retrieved from http://www.journalism.org/2014/03/26/ 8-key-takeaways-about-social-media-and-news/.

ACKNOWLEDGMENTS

During the final moments of my last broadcast at CBS News, tears welled up in my eyes. Journalists are not supposed to show emotion, so I did everything I could to keep the tears from rolling down my cheeks. As my voice cracked, I closed out the show by saying two things I wanted on record: While viewers only saw me each morning, the shows I anchored were the result of hard work from a big team of absolutely amazing people, and to that team I would be forever grateful. And while I was thankful for my colleagues' brilliance, I was even more grateful for their friendship. Without both, the shows would not have been possible. The same holds true for this book. It is only with the incredible talent and support from the following people, and countless others, that this book could have come into being.

I am deeply grateful to my family for all their love and support. My husband, Shawn Achor, for more than I could ever hope to put down here on paper. You are my love, intellectual crush, fellow researcher, and best friend. Your support through this process has been unreal. I am an incredibly lucky woman for not only having married a man I admire but also finding one who is so full of love (and constantly acts on that love with everyone) that he inspires me to love more deeply every day.

Leonardo Grant Achor, aka #babyleo, our son, for your hugs and cuddles and excitement as you discover the world. Bearing witness to your awe-inspiring growth and development as a human being has deepened my understanding of the human potential to broadcast happiness. You have shown me it is not that we can't broadcast happiness—we are born full of joy—we just need to learn to consciously and fully return to it and thereby return to love.

Dan and Barbara Gielan, my parents, for your wisdom and guidance. Many of the ideas in this book grew from seeds planted by you. I deeply admire you both and will be forever thankful for the love and opportunities you have given me all these years.

David and Jenna Gielan, my brother and sister-in-law, for your support and comic relief. It is incredible how sometimes a "little" brother can be such a wise teacher to his big sis.

Amy and Bobo Blankson for wrestling with life's big topics with Shawn and me in a way that creates growth. And my nieces, Ana, Gabri, and Kobi—I love you girls!

Jordan and Kelci Brock, who taught me that it is possible to turn friends into family through love and intention.

Our team at GoodThink, half of which has already been named because we are a family business. Shawn, Amy, Jordan, Hannah Costner, Alexis Bierman Roberts, Cathy McCain, and Brandy Bisbocci. I am grateful beyond measure for your insights, feedback, and support.

Alecia Pulman Kimchy, Ann Browning, Sarah Moga, Courtney Friel, Betsy Korona, Natali Del Conte Morris, Debbi Bourke, Jacey Bloom Greece, Amanda Berndt, Becky Kozdron Dumcum, and Ilana Klein for being amazing friends. Even though we are separated by distance, you hold a special place in my heart.

Glenn Yeffeth, Jennifer Canzoneri, Vy Tran, Adrienne Lang, Monica Lowry, Alicia Kania, and the rest of the team at Ben-Bella Books. You have been truly incredible partners through this process. For anyone looking for a boutique publishing house that provides personal attention, I highly recommend BenBella Books.

Jenny Canzoneri, Holli Catchpole, Michele Rubino Wallace, Marsha Horshok, Cassie Glasgow, Kim Stark—the team at

SpeakersOffice in California that flawlessly handles all our back-office logistics while keeping things fun.

Michael Wright from Garson & Wright Public Relations. Thank you for singing the praises of this book and helping us get the messages within it international attention.

Arianna Huffington and Danny Shea for your forward-thinking, bold call for journalists to report more solutions-focused news and your excitement in partnering with our research institute to investigate the effects of positive and negative news on the brain.

All my friends from FOX News Chicago—too many to name—for an amazing experience in the Windy City and for welcoming me back after CBS to broadcast positive psychology segments on the morning show.

My friends from CBS News, including Anlynn Truong, Brian Applegate, Tony Dipolvere, Joe Gelosi, Jenn Eaker, Norman Gittleson, James McGrath, Chris Easley, Erika Wortham, Myra Zuleta, Mike Mancini, Greg Carlson, Bob Meyer, Russ Mitchell, Vera Gibbons, Carol Story, and Lauren Danza. Thank you for your excitement while producing Happy Week and the other positive, solutions-focused segments we put together.

Kym Yancey, Deborah Heisz, Donna Stokes, and the rest of the team from Live Happy for your commitment to walking the walk and broadcasting happiness as a way of life. Thank you for showcasing our positive psychology research in such a beautiful way.

Ernie Anastos, Gerry Richman, Colleen Steward, Kathy Caprino, and Kristen Adams for your work bringing broadcasting happiness research to television. You are shining examples of the transformative journalist that I write about in the Journalist Manifesto at the end of this book.

Lisa Weiss, Laura Berger, Amanda Cash, and the rest of the SuperSoulers at HARPO for broadcasting happiness in its truest, most spiritual form.

Tiffany Sun, Ofer Leidner, Ran Zilca, and the rest of the team at Happify for partnering with GoodThink to turn our happiness research into an online application to create and sustain a positive mindset. The work you are doing is truly at the forefront of the field of applied positive psychology.

Greg Ray, Greg Kaiser, Kevin Karaffa, and Mark McDonald for being supportive of this book from the beginning and for bringing our positive psychology research to life at major organizations in such an exciting and transformative way.

Gary Baker, president of Nationwide Brokerage Solutions, who let us turn his company into a Petri dish to test happiness strategies and together realize such a compelling business case for putting happiness research into practice.

My friends from Google—Li-Ming Pu, Catherine Brown, Anna-Maria Kourkoulakos, and Sarah McGuire—for championing happiness research at the highest levels of the company. Holding space for important conversations on work and happiness shifts thinking and transforms lives, and that is what you do on a regular basis.

Dr. Karen Panetta, my professor of Computer Engineering at Tufts University, a powerhouse in a male-dominated field, who is creating a positive ripple effect in her classroom and the world. You are a role model and friend.

Marty Seligman for founding the field of positive psychology and doing research that is so fascinating it lured me away from national television and into the lab to work and study alongside you. You have left an indelible mark on the world of psychology. We are just starting to comprehend the magnitude of the positive ripple effect positive psychology is having on global well-being.

Alia Crum, Libby Benson, Peggy Kern, and Kristen Merkitch for your commitment to positive psychology research, both conducting and living it. I am so thankful to have you as fellow researchers and friends.

My MAPP friends, especially my GGSs. As classmates during our master's program in positive psychology at the University of Pennsylvania, I learned from each one of you tremendously. May your lights shine bright and continue to spark transformation in the rest of the world. With each paper you publish, presentation you give, initiative you start, radio broadcast you do, patient you treat, news report you write, research study you conduct, or person you talk to about positive psychology, you are transformative ambassadors and broadcasters of this research. I am thankful to have the chance to be part of this incredible group of human beings.

Kenny Lindner and Shari Freis from Ken Lindner & Associates. You transformed what I thought of broadcast agents, becoming my good friends. I am deeply appreciative to you for what you did to help make the story near the beginning of this book a possibility.

Elizabeth Lesser for welcoming me into the Omega Institute family and being a compass at a time when I was looking for direction on how to best serve the world. You and your work continue to be such an inspiration to me personally.

Joel and Victoria Osteen, pastors of Lakewood Church in Houston. Your positive messages of love and triumph broadcasted online have helped keep me energized through this writing process. May our paths cross sometime soon so I can thank you both in person.

And to the thousands of people who have watched my shows or attended my talks over the years and shared your stories with me—thank you! Please keep sharing with me all the ways big and small that you bring this research to life and the positive ripple effect it has on your work, family, and community. It's those stories that serve as inspiration to others to choose to broadcast happiness as well.

ABOUT THE AUTHOR

Michelle Gielan is the founder of the Institute for Applied Positive Research. She works with Fortune 500 companies and schools to raise employee engagement, productivity, and happiness at work. Michelle is a managing partner at GoodThink, a positive psychology consulting firm, and she holds a Master's of Applied Positive Psychology from the University of Pennsylvania. Michelle graduated cum laude in Computer Engineering.

Michelle is an executive producer of *The Happiness Advantage* special on PBS. She formerly served as the anchor of two national newscasts at CBS News, as well as a correspondent for *The Early Show*. Her research and advice have received attention from Forbes, *USA Today*, CNN, FOX, and NPR.